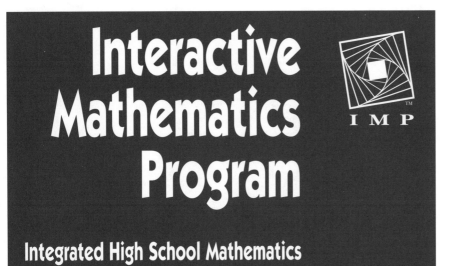

Interactive Mathematics Program

Integrated High School Mathematics

YEAR 1

The Overland Trail

Dan Fendel and Diane Resek
with
Lynne Alper and Sherry Fraser

KEY CURRICULUM PRESS
Innovators in Mathematics Education

This material is based upon work
supported by the
National Science Foundation
under award number
ESI-9255262. Any opinions,
findings, and conclusions or
recommendations expressed
in this publication are those of
the authors and do not necessarily
reflect the views of the
National Science Foundation.

™ Interactive Mathematics Program,
IMP, and the IMP logo are trademarks
of Key Curriculum Press.

Key Curriculum Press
P.O. Box 2304
Berkeley, California 94702
editorial@keypress.com
http://www.keypress.com

10 9 8 7 6 5 4 3   00 99 98 97
ISBN 1-55953-253-X
Printed in the
United States of America

Project Editor
Casey FitzSimons

Additional Editorial Development
Dan Bennett, Bill Finzer, Crystal Mills

Editorial Production
Caroline Ayres, Debbie Cogan,
Greer Lleuad, Jason Luz

Editorial Assistants
Jeff Gammon, Romy Snyder

Teacher Reviews
Dave Calhoun, John Chart, Dwight Fuller,
Donna Gaarder, Dan Johnson, Jean Klanica,
Cathie Thompson

Multicultural Reviews
Edward Castillo, Ph.D., Sonoma State University
Genevieve Lau, Ph.D., Skyline College

Cover and Interior Design
Terry Lockman
Lumina Designworks

Cover Photography and Cover Illustration
Hillary Turner and Tom Fowler

Production
Luis Shein

Production Coordination
Susan Parini

Technical Graphics
Greg Reeves

Illustration
Tom Fowler, Evangelia Philippidis,
Diane Varner, Martha Weston,
April Goodman Willy

Publisher
Steven Rasmussen

Editorial Director
John Bergez

Acknowledgments

Many people have contributed to the development of the IMP curriculum, including the hundreds of teachers and many thousands of students who used preliminary versions of the materials. Of course, there is no way to thank all of them individually, but the IMP directors want to give some special acknowledgments.

We want to give extraordinary thanks to the following people who played unique roles in the development of the curriculum.

- **Bill Finzer** was one of the original directors of IMP before going on to different pastures. He helped shape the overall vision of the program, and worked on drafts of several Year 1 units.

- **Matt Bremer** did the initial revision of every unit after its pilot testing. Each unit of the curriculum also underwent extensive focus group reexamination after being taught for several years, and Matt did the rewrite of many units following the focus groups. He has read every word of everyone else's revisions as well, and has contributed tremendous insight through his understanding of high school students and the high school classroom.

- **Mary Jo Cittadino** became a high school student once again during the piloting of the curriculum, attending class daily and doing all the class activities, homework, and POWs. Because of this experience, her contributions to focus groups had a unique perspective. This is a good place to thank her also for her contributions to IMP as Network Coordinator for California. In that capacity, she has visited many IMP classrooms and answered thousands of questions from parents, teachers, and administrators.

- **Lori Green** left the classroom as a regular teacher after the 1989–90 school year and became a traveling resource for IMP classroom teachers. In that role, she has seen more classes using the curriculum than we can count, and the insights from her classroom observations have been a valuable resource in her work in the focus groups.

- **Celia Stevenson** developed the charming and witty graphics that graced the pre-publication versions of all the IMP units.

Several people played particular roles in the development of this unit, *The Overland Trail:*

- Matt Bremer, Janice Bussey, Donna Gaarder, Lori Green, and Tom Zimmerman helped us create the version of *The Overland Trail* that was pilot tested during 1989–90. They not only taught the unit in their classrooms that year, but also read and commented on early drafts, tested out almost all the activities during workshops that preceded the teaching, and then came back after teaching the unit with insights that contributed to the initial revision.

- Janice Bussey, Margaret DeArmond, George Kirchner, Leigh Ann McCready, and Robin Rice joined Matt Bremer, Mary Jo Cittadino, and Lori Green for the focus group on *The Overland Trail* in August, 1993. Their contributions built on several years of IMP teaching, including at least two years teaching this unit, and their work led to the development of the last field-test version of the unit.

- Dan Branham, Dave Calhoun, John Chart, Steve Hansen, Mary Hunter, Caran Resciniti, Gwennyth Trice, and Julie Walker field tested the post-focus group version of *The Overland Trail* during 1994–95. Dave and John met with us when the teaching of the unit was finished to share their experiences. Their feedback helped shape the final version that now appears.

In creating this program, we needed help in many dimensions other than writing curriculum and giving support to teachers.

The National Science Foundation has been the primary sponsor of the Interactive Mathematics Program. We want to thank NSF for its ongoing support, and especially want to extend our personal thanks to Dr. Margaret Cozzens, Director of NSF's Division of Elementary, Secondary, and Informal Education, for her encouragement and her faith in our efforts.

We also want to acknowledge here the initial support for curriculum development from the California Postsecondary Education Commission and the San Francisco Foundation, and the major support for dissemination from the Noyce Foundation and the David and Lucile Packard Foundation.

Keeping all of our work going required the help of a first-rate office staff. This group of talented and hard-working individuals worked tirelessly on many tasks, such as sending out units, keeping the books balanced, helping us get our message out to the public, and handling communications with schools, teachers, and administrators. We greatly appreciate their dedication.

- Barbara Ford—Secretary

- Tony Gillies—Project Manager

- Marianne Smith—Publicist

- Linda Witnov—Outreach Coordinator

We want to thank Dr. Norman Webb, of the Wisconsin Center for Education Research, for his leadership in our evaluation program, and our Evaluation Advisory Board, whose expertise was so valuable in that aspect of our work.

- David Clarke, University of Melbourne

- Robert Davis, Rutgers University

- George Hein, Lesley College

- Mark St. John, Inverness Research Associates

IMP National Advisory Board

Finally, we want to thank Steve Rasmussen, President of Key Curriculum Press, Casey FitzSimons, Key's Project Editor for the IMP curriculum, and the many others at Key whose work turned our ideas and words into published form.

Dan Fendel   Diane Resek   Lynne Alper   Sherry Fraser

The Interactive Mathematics Program

What is the Interactive Mathematics Program?

The Interactive Mathematics Program (IMP) is a growing collaboration of mathematicians, teacher-educators, and teachers who have been working together since 1989 on both curriculum development and teacher professional development.

What is the IMP curriculum?

IMP has created a four-year program of problem-based mathematics that replaces the traditional Algebra I–Geometry–Algebra II/Trigonometry–Precalculus sequence and that is designed to exemplify the curriculum reform called for in the *Curriculum and Evaluation Standards* of the National Council of Teachers of Mathematics.

The IMP curriculum integrates traditional material with additional topics recommended by the NCTM *Standards*, such as statistics, probability, curve fitting, and matrix algebra. Although every IMP unit has a specific mathematical focus (for instance, similar triangles), most units are structured around a central problem and bring in other topics as needed to solve that problem, rather than narrowly restricting the mathematical content. Ideas that are developed in one unit are generally revisited and deepened in one or more later units.

For which students is the IMP curriculum intended?

The IMP curriculum is for all students. One of IMP's goals is to make the learning of a core mathematics curriculum accessible to everyone. Toward that end, we have designed the program for use with heterogeneous classes. We provide you with a varied collection of supplemental problems to give you the flexibility to meet individual student needs.

Teacher Phyllis Quick confers with a group of students.

How is the IMP classroom different?

When you use the IMP curriculum, your role changes from "imparter of knowledge" to observer and facilitator. You ask challenging questions. You do not give all the answers but you prod students to do their own thinking, to make generalizations, and to go beyond the immediate problem by asking themselves "What if?"

The IMP curriculum gives students many opportunities to write about their mathematical thinking, to reflect on what they have done, and to make oral presentations to each other about their work. In IMP, your assessment of students becomes integrated with learning, and you evaluate students in a variety of ways, including class participation, daily homework assignments, Problems of the Week, portfolios, and unit assessments. The IMP *Teaching Handbook* provides many practical suggestions for teachers on how to get the best possible results using this curriculum in *your* classroom.

What is in Year 1 of the IMP curriculum?

Year 1 of the IMP curriculum contains five units.

Patterns

The primary purpose of this unit is to introduce students to ways of working on and thinking about mathematics that may be new to them. In a sense, the unit is an overall introduction to the IMP curriculum, which involves changes for many students in how they learn mathematics and what they think of as mathematics. The main mathematical ideas of the unit include function tables, the use of variables, positive and negative numbers, and some basic geometrical concepts.

The Game of Pig

A dice game called Pig forms the core of this unit. Playing and analyzing Pig involves students in a wide variety of mathematical activities. The basic problem for students is to find an optimum strategy for playing the game. In order to find a good strategy and prove that it is optimum, students work with the concept of expected value and develop a mathematical analysis for the game based on an area model for probability.

The Overland Trail

This unit looks at the mid-nineteenth century western migration across what is now the United States in terms of the many mathematical relationships involved. These relationships involve planning what to take on the 2400-mile trek, estimating the cost of the move, studying rates of consumption and of travel, and estimating the time to reach the final goal. A major mathematical focus of the unit is the use of equations, tables, and graphs to describe real-life situations.

The Pit and the Pendulum

In Edgar Allan Poe's story, *The Pit and the Pendulum,* a prisoner is tied down while a pendulum with a sharp blade slowly descends. If the prisoner does not act, he will be killed by the pendulum. Students read an excerpt from the story, and are presented with the problem of whether the prisoner would have enough time to escape. To resolve this question, they construct pendulums and conduct experiments. In the process, they are introduced to the concepts of normal distribution and standard deviation as tools for determining whether a change in one variable really does affect another. They use graphing calculators to learn about quadratic equations and to explore curve fitting. Finally, after deriving a theoretical answer to the pendulum problem, students actually build a thirty-foot pendulum to test their theory.

Shadows

The central question of this unit is, "How can you predict the length of a shadow?" The unit moves quickly from this concrete problem to the geometric concept of similarity. Students work with a variety of approaches to come to an understanding of similar polygons, especially similar triangles. Then they return to the problem of the shadow, applying their knowledge of similar triangles and using informal methods for solving proportions, to develop a general formula. In the last part of the unit, students learn about the three primary trigonometric functions—sine, cosine, and tangent—as they apply to acute angles, and they apply these functions to problems of finding heights and distances.

How do the four years of the IMP curriculum fit together?

The four years of the IMP curriculum form an integrated sequence through which students can learn the mathematics they will need, both for further education and on the job. Although the organization of the IMP curriculum is very different from the traditional Algebra I–Geometry–Algebra II/Trigonometry–Precalculus sequence, the important mathematical ideas are all there.

Here are some examples of how both traditional concepts and topics new to the high school curriculum are developed.

Linear equations

In Year 1 of the IMP curriculum, students develop an intuitive foundation about algebraic thinking, including the use of variables, which they build on throughout the program. In the Year 2 unit *Solve It!,* students use the concept of equivalent equations to see how to solve any linear equation in a single variable. Later in Year 2, in a unit called *Cookies* (about maximizing profits for a bakery), they solve pairs of linear equations in two variables, using both algebraic and geometric methods. In the Year 3 unit *Meadows or Malls?,* they extend those ideas to systems with more than two variables, and see how to use matrices and the technology of graphing calculators to solve such systems.

Measurement and the Pythagorean theorem

Measurement, including area and volume, is one of the fundamental topics in geometry. The Pythagorean theorem is one of the most important geometric principles ever discovered. In the Year 2 unit *Do Bees Build It Best?,* students combine these ideas with their knowledge of similarity (from the Year 1 unit *Shadows*) to see why the hexagonal prism of the bees' honeycomb design is the most efficient regular prism possible. Students also use the Pythagorean theorem in later units, applying it to develop principles like the distance formula in coordinate geometry.

Trigonometric functions

In traditional programs, the trigonometric functions are introduced in the eleventh or twelfth grade. In the IMP curriculum, students begin working with trigonometry in Year 1 (in *Shadows*), using right-triangle trigonometry in several units (including *Do Bees Build It Best?*) in Years 2 and 3. In the Year 4 unit *High Dive,* they extend trigonometry from right triangles to circular functions, in the context of a circus act in which a performer falls from a Ferris wheel into a moving tub of water. (In *High Dive,* students also learn principles of physics, developing laws for falling objects and finding the vertical and horizontal components of velocity.)

Standard deviation and the binomial distribution

Standard deviation and the binomial distribution are major tools in the study of probability and statistics. *The Game of Pig* gets students started by building a firm understanding of concepts of probability and the phenomenon of experimental variation. Later in Year 1 (in *The Pit and the Pendulum*), they use standard deviation to see that the period of a pendulum is determined primarily by its length. In Year 2, they compare standard deviation with the chi-square test in examining whether a set of data is statistically significant. In *Pennant Fever* (Year 3), students use the binomial distribution to evaluate a team's chances of winning the baseball championship, and in *The Pollster's Dilemma* (Year 4), students tie many of these ideas together in the central limit theorem, seeing how the margin of error and the level of certainty for an election poll depend on its size.

Does the program work?

The IMP curriculum has been thoroughly field-tested by hundreds of classroom teachers around the country. Their enthusiasm comes from the success they have seen in their own classrooms with their own students. For those who measure success by test scores, we mention that repeated studies have proved that IMP students do at least as well as students in traditional mathematics classes on tests like the SAT, even though IMP students spend far less time than traditional students on the algebra and geometry skills emphasized by these tests. With the time saved, IMP students learn topics such as statistics that other students don't see until they reach college.

But one of our proudest achievements is that IMP students are excited about mathematics, as shown by the fact that they take more mathematics courses in high school than their counterparts in traditional programs. We think this is because they see that mathematics can be relevant to their own lives. If so, then the program works.

Dan Fendel
Diane Resek
Lynne Alper
Sherry Fraser

Note to Students

These pages in the student book welcome students to the program.

You are about to begin an adventure in mathematics, an adventure organized around interesting, complex problems. The concepts you learn grow out of what is needed to solve those problems.

This curriculum was developed by the Interactive Mathematics Program (IMP), a collaboration of teachers, teacher-educators, and mathematicians who have been working together since 1989 to reform the way high school mathematics is taught. About one hundred thousand students and five hundred teachers used these materials before they were published. Their experiences, reactions, and ideas have been incorporated into the final version you now hold.

Our goal is to give you the mathematics you need to succeed in this changing world. We want to present mathematics to you in a manner that reflects how mathematics is used and reflects the different ways people work and learn together. Through this perspective on mathematics, you will be prepared both for continued study of mathematics in college and for the world of work.

This book contains the various assignments that will be your work during Year 1 of the program. As you will see, these assignments incorporate ideas from many branches of mathematics, including algebra, geometry, probability, graphing, statistics, and trigonometry. Other topics will come up in later parts of this four-year program. Rather than present each of these areas separately, we have integrated

Interactive Mathematics Program

them and presented them in meaningful contexts so that you'll see how they relate to one another and to our world.

Each unit in this four-year program has a central problem or theme, and focuses on several major mathematical ideas. Within each unit, the material is organized for teaching purposes into "Days," with a homework assignment for each day. (Your class may not follow this schedule exactly, especially if it doesn't meet every day.)

At the end of the main material for each unit, you will find a set of "supplemental problems." These problems provide additional opportunities for you to work with ideas from the unit, either to strengthen your understanding of the core material or to explore new ideas related to the unit.

Although the IMP program is not organized into courses called Algebra, Geometry, and so on, you will be learning all the essential mathematical concepts that are part of those traditional courses. You will also be learning concepts from branches of mathematics—especially statistics and probability— that are not part of a traditional high school program.

To accomplish this goal, you will have to be an active learner. Simply reading this book will not allow you to achieve your goal, because the book does not teach directly. Your role as a mathematics student will be to experiment, investigate, ask questions, make and test conjectures, and reflect, and then communicate your ideas and conclusions both verbally and in writing. You will do some work in collaboration with your fellow students, just as users of mathematics in the real world often work in teams. At other times, you will be working on your own.

We hope you will enjoy the challenge of this new way of learning mathematics and will see mathematics in a new light.

Dan Fendel   Diane Resek   Lynne Alper   Sherry Fraser

Finding What You Need

We designed this guide to help you find what you need amid all the information it provides. Each of the following components has a special treatment in the layout of the guide.

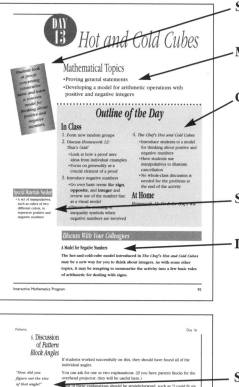

Synopsis of the Day: The key idea or activity for each day is summarized in a brief sentence or two.

Mathematical Topics: Mathematical issues for the day are presented in a bulleted list.

Outline of the Day: Under the *In Class* heading, the outline summarizes the activities for the day, which are keyed to numbered headings in the discussion. Daily homework assignments and Problems of the Week are listed under the *At Home* heading.

Special Materials Needed: Special items needed in the classroom for each day are bulleted here.

Discuss With Your Colleagues: This section highlights topics that you may want to discuss with your peers.

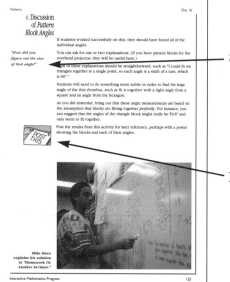

Suggested Questions: These are specific questions that you might ask during an activity or discussion to promote student insight or to determine whether students understand an idea. The appropriateness of these questions generally depends on what students have already developed or presented on their own.

Post This: The *Post This* icon indicates items that you may want to display in the classroom.

Icons for Student Written Products

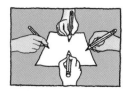

Single Group report

Individual reports

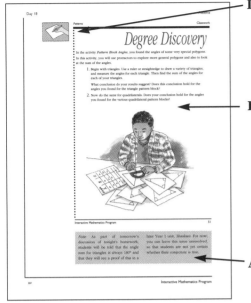

Icons for Student Written Products: For each group activity, there is an icon suggesting a single group report, individual reports, or no report at all. If graphs are included, the icon indicates this as well. (The graph icons do not appear in every unit.)

Embedded Student Pages: Embedded within the pages of the teacher guide are reduced-size copies of the pages from the student book. These reduced student pages include the "transition pages" that appear occasionally within each unit to summarize each portion of the unit and to prepare students for what is coming. Having all of these student pages in the teacher guide is a helpful way for you to see things from the students' perspective.

Asides: These are ideas outside the main thrust of a discussion. They include background information for teachers, refinements or subtle points that may only be of interest to some students, ways to help fill in gaps in understanding the main ideas, and suggestions about when to bring in a particular concept.

Additional Information

Here is a brief outline of other tools we have included to assist you and make both the teaching and the learning experience more rewarding.

Glossary: This section, which is found at the back of the book, gives the definitions of important terms for all of Year 1 for easy reference. The same glossary appears in the student book.

Appendix A: Supplemental Problems: This appendix contains a variety of interesting additional activities for the unit, for teachers who would like to supplement material found in the regular classroom problems. These additional activities are of two types—*reinforcements,* which help increase student understanding of concepts that are central to the unit, and *extensions,* which allow students to explore ideas beyond the basic unit.

Appendix B: Blackline Masters: For each unit, this appendix contains materials you can reproduce that are not available in the student book and that will be helpful to teacher and student alike. They include the end-of-unit assessments as well as such items as diagrams from which you can make transparencies. Semester assessments for Year 1 are included in *The Overland Trail* (for first semester) and *Shadows* (for second semester).

Single group graph

Individual graphs

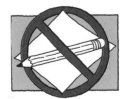

No report at all

Year 1 IMP Units

Contents

"The Overland Trail" Overview

Summary of the Unit

The westward migration across the United States in the mid-nineteenth century involved whole families packing up their earthly goods and going in covered wagons on a six- to eight-month journey across largely uncharted plains, deserts, and mountains.

This unit uses the long trip from Missouri to California as a backdrop for studying numerical relationships and, in particular, linear relationships. These relationships grow out of such considerations as planning what to take on the trip, figuring out how much food will be needed, and estimating the time to reach the final goal. Interspersed with problems set in the historical period of the Overland Trail are many problems involving current-day settings.

The unit has several mathematical themes, including the use of variables and graphs.

Variables are used in the unit to write formulas and equations in order to express relationships. Formulas are seen as a way to generalize the arithmetic of specific situations, and are often developed by analyzing the pattern of arithmetic used in specific cases. The focus in this unit is on strengthening students' intuition about the meaning of variables, without getting sidetracked by the symbol manipulation that is generally associated with algebra.

Graphs also play an important role in the unit. Students begin by looking at unscaled graphs that relate two quantities, interpreting the graphs in terms of the problem situation; they also create graphs based on problem situations. They then consider the issues involved in adding scaling to the graphs. They examine the relationship between a graph, an equation, and a table of data, and learn how each of these can be used to represent a problem situation. Students draw graphs by hand and with graphing calculators, and use their graphs to interpret data and to make predictions.

Another aim of the unit is to enable students to deal with ambiguity. Many of the situations presented do not have crisp, clean mathematical formulations, and students are asked to clarify their assumptions as they interpret data or work with complex problem situations. The problems should help students learn that many questions that arise in real-life situations are not solved by looking for the one right answer. They will see that they need to think about the situation, decide what simplifying assumptions need to be made, and then solve the problem based on those assumptions.

At the beginning of the unit, each group of students creates four Overland Trail families, according to specific guidelines. They then follow these families along the trail, overseeing their supplies, calculating their time on the trail, and even confronting the possible death of family members.

In terms of the geographical setting of the long journey, the unit breaks down roughly like this.

- Days 1–4: Setting up Overland Trail families

- Days 5–7: Preparing for the first leg of the journey

- Days 8–10: Traveling from Westport, Missouri, to Fort Laramie, Wyoming

- Days 11–16: Stopping in Fort Laramie and preparing for the next leg of the journey

- Days 17–19: Traveling from Fort Laramie, Wyoming, to Fort Hall, Idaho

- Days 20–27: Traveling from Fort Hall, Idaho, to California

- Day 28: Arrival in California

The last four days of the unit are set aside for presentations of the final Problem of the Week (POW), assembling portfolios, taking end-of-unit assessments, and summing up.

In terms of mathematical themes, the unit follows the outline below (once the initial planning material is introduced).

- Days 7–10 focus on the use and meaning of variables.

- Days 11–14 deal primarily with the drawing of graphs from both descriptive information and algebraic equations, including the appropriate use of scales and the connections between situations, graphs, tables, and algebraic rules.

- Days 15–18 focus on interpreting graphs and using them to make predictions and to solve problems.

- Days 19–21 introduce the use of graphing calculators to plot data and to graph equations, and include the use of zoom and trace techniques.

- Days 22–24 focus on the use of a linear equation to represent a situation and the use of a graph to help find solutions for problems involving two linear conditions.

- Days 25–28 apply many of the ideas developed earlier to solve problems involving different kinds of rates.

Working with the History Teacher

This unit provides an excellent opportunity for interdisciplinary study. You and colleagues in the mathematics department may want to meet with social studies faculty to see how students' work on this unit can be coordinated with work students are doing in history.

Resources

The following books were used as source material in preparing this unit. They may be helpful in providing students with further information about the era in which the unit is set.

- Ralph K. Andrist, *The Long Death* (New York: Collier Books, Macmillan Publishing, 1964)

- Herbert Eaton, *The Overland Trail to California in 1852* (New York: Capricorn Books, G. P. Putnam's Sons, 1974)

- John Mack Faragher, *Women and Men on the Overland Trail* (New Haven: Yale University Press, 1979)

- Gwinn Harris Heap, *Central Route to the Pacific* (New York: Arno Press, 1981; reprint of the 1854 edition published by J. B. Lippincott Co.)

- James Hewitt, *Eye-Witnesses to Wagon Trains West* (New York: Charles Scribner's Sons, 1973)

- Kenneth Holmes, *Covered Wagon Women, Diaries and Letters from the Western Trails, 1840–1890*, vol. 1 (Glendale, CA: The Arthur H. Clark Co., 1983)

- William Loren Katz, *Black People Who Made the Old West* (Trenton, NJ: African World Press, 1992)

- Savoie Lotinville, *Life of George Bent* (Norman, OK: University of Oklahoma Press, 1968)

- Peter Nabakov, ed., *Native American Testimony*, (New York: Penguin Books, 1991)

- Lillian Schlissel, *Women's Diaries of the Westward Journey* (New York: Schocken Books, 1983)

- George R. Stewart, *The California Trail, An Epic with Many Heroes* (New York: McGraw-Hill Book Co., 1962)

Your high school or local library may have these and other books on the period for you to use as resources.

You may also want to make use of one or more videos.

- *How the West Was Lost*, available from the Public Broadcasting System

- *The Donner Party*, available from the Public Broadcasting System

- *Gone West*, available from Social Studies School Service, 10200 Jefferson Blvd., Rm. 121, PO Box 802, Culver City, CA 90232-0802.

Concepts and Skills

The major mathematical themes of this unit include the organization and use of data and the representation and interpretation of information symbolically and graphically. Considerable attention is given to the connections between situations, graphs, In-Out tables, and algebraic rules.

The main concepts and skills that students will encounter and practice during the course of this unit can be summarized by category as shown below.

Data and decision-making

- Compiling and organizing data

- Creating examples that fit a set of constraints

- Interpreting ambiguous problems

- Finding numbers that fit several conditions

- Making estimates and plans for various situations

- Using tables of information and lines of best fit to make predictions and estimates

Graphs and modeling

- Interpreting graphs intuitively and using graphs intuitively to represent situations

- Making graphs from tabular information

- Quantifying graphs with appropriate scales

- Using graphs to represent equations and writing equations that describe graphs

- Making graphs on a graphing calculator

- Using zoom and trace facilities to get information from a graphing calculator

- Finding lines of best fit intuitively

- Using the point of intersection of graphs to satisfy two conditions

- Working with rate problems of various types
- Using multiple representations—graphs, In-Out tables, and algebraic relationships—to describe situations

Algorithms, variables and notation

- Developing numerical algorithms for problem situations
- Expressing algorithms in words and symbols
- Interpreting algebraic expressions in words using summary phrases
- Developing meaningful algebraic expressions
- Using subscript notation
- Solving equations for one variable in terms of others
- Expressing linear approximations to data algebraically
- Solving problems involving two linear conditions

Other concepts and skills are developed in connection with Problems of the Week.

Materials

You will need to provide the materials listed below during the course of this unit (in addition to standard materials, such as graphing calculators, transparencies, chart paper, marking pens, and so forth).

- Dice (two per group)
- Optional: Clear straightedges (useful for finding lines of best fit)
- A wall-size map of the United States
- Folders in which groups can keep information about their Overland Trail families

Grading

The IMP *Teaching Handbook* contains general guidelines about how to grade students in an IMP class. You will probably want to check daily that students have done their homework, and include regular completion of homework as part of students' grades. Your grading scheme will probably also include Problems of the Week, the unit portfolio, and the end-of-unit assessments.

Because you will not be able to read thoroughly every assignment that students turn in, you will need to select certain assignments to read carefully and to base grades on. Here are some suggestions:

- *Homework 2: Hats for the Families*
- *Homework 7: Laced Travelers*
- *Homework 11: Graph Sketches*

- *Homework 13: Situations, Graphs, Tables, and Rules*
- *Who Will Make It?* (Day 17)
- *Homework 23: More "Fair Share for Hired Hands"*
- *Catching Up by Saturday Night* (Day 27)

If you want to base your grading on a larger number of tasks, there are many other homework assignments, class activities, and oral presentations you can use.

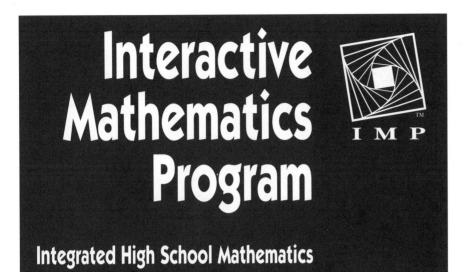

Interactive Mathematics Program

Integrated High School Mathematics

IMP

YEAR 1

The Overland Trail

The Overland Trail

A Journey Back in Time

This unit follows the nineteenth-century movement of settlers from Missouri to California. You will see ways in which these settlers may have used mathematics as they undertook a trip that lasted several months and almost two thousand miles.

This page in the student book introduces Days 1 through 6.

You will encounter some very important mathematical ideas—such as graphs, different uses of variables, lines of best fit, and rate problems—as you travel across the continent. You'll also learn interesting history as you and your fictional family encounter some real-life participants in your travels.

Stanley Pinkston sets the stage for the long journey west.

Families on the Overland Trail

Students are introduced to the historical setting of the unit.

Mathematical Topics

- Introduction to the historical context of the unit

Outline of the Day

In Class

1. Form new groups that will last throughout the unit
2. Introduce the setting of the unit
3. Have students read *The Overland Trail*

   (Optional) Students watch a video about the historical period

4. Have students do focused-free writing on a topic related to the historical setting

At Home

Homework 1: Just Like Today

Special Materials Needed

- A wall-size map of the United States (for use throughout the unit)

1. Form New Groups

Put students into groups, as described in the IMP *Teaching Handbook.*

Students will stay in the same group for the entire length of this unit. On Days 2 and 3, groups will create families that travel on the Overland Trail, and they will follow these families throughout the unit. For example, they will make planning decisions for these families (Days 5 and 6) that will take effect later in the unit. The aim is for the group to imagine themselves as a team traveling together along the trail.

We recommend that you let students know that they will be working with the same people for a while.

2. Introduction to the Unit

Today's main goal is for students to begin to get a sense of the history surrounding the Overland Trail, which is a collective name for a group of trails that led from Missouri to the West.

Use a large classroom map to show students the route of the California Trail, which began in Westport, Missouri (near present-day Kansas City), and ended at Sutter's Fort, California.

Most of this trail was originally known as the Emigrant Trail, or Oregon Trail, and it ended near what is now Portland, Oregon. The California Trail split from the Oregon Trail west of Fort Hall, which was located in what is now Pocatello, Idaho.

As historical background, you can identify the Native American nations through whose land the trail ran. The trail began in Shawnee, Kansa, Lenni-Lenape (Delaware), Cheyenne, and Arapaho territory. The Dakota nation held the land that is now Nebraska and part of Wyoming. The Shoshone, Assiniboin, and Crow nations held the land of present-day Wyoming and Idaho. The Oregon Trail cut through Choppunish (Nez Percé), Flathead, Yakima, and Chinook territory. Some 300 different nations, including the Modoc, Washo, Maidu, Pomo, and Miwok, held territory in what is now California.

You can mark these Native American nations on the map, where the trail crosses their lands. Also, you can identify the modern-day states that the trail passes through—Missouri, Kansas, Nebraska, Wyoming, Idaho, Nevada, and California.

By the mid-1800s, the United States government had appropriated Native American lands in the East and Midwest and moved whole Native American nations westward. Prior to 1840, the government "reserved" the land known as the Great Plains for those displaced peoples, calling it Indian Country. The established boundary of Indian Country started in the South at the edge of the Republic of Texas and ran north along the western boundaries of Arkansas and Missouri, across the northern border of Missouri roughly to the Mississippi River. It followed the Mississippi into Minnesota before cutting across Wisconsin on an irregular line to Lake Michigan. (The map for 1830 in *Homework 15: Broken Promises* shows approximately this same boundary.)

The land was pledged to Native Americans to have and to hold forever. The United States government liked to use the phrase "as long as waters flow and the grass shall grow" in its treaties. This land was to be the final home for the displaced tribes from the East and for the existing tribes of the plain. Between 1778 and 1868, Native American nations and the

United States government signed more than 400 treaties or agreements. The United States government broke every one of them. (The shameful government record of broken treaties is referred to in *Homework 15: Broken Promises.)*

There are references in the unit to the devastating effects of western migration on Native Americans, but this devastation cannot be overstated. Any stories that you know or find will no doubt add more depth to the unit.

Students will be more engaged in the unit if they can make a connection with people who made the journey. This connection can be strengthened by looking at a video depicting the era, either now or at a later point during the unit. (This is a good activity for a day when there is a substitute teacher.)

Similarly, try to bring in photos and drawings of the era so that students have visual images to relate to.

- *Note on historical accuracy and inaccuracy*

The geographical information in this unit is accurate to the best of our knowledge, and the times given for various sections of the journey are reasonable estimates based on sources from and about the period.

Information on prices from the period is based on sources where so noted, but otherwise may not bear any resemblance to actual values at the time.

The following persons, whose names appear in the activities, were real individuals, and the information related about them is drawn from books listed in the bibliography.

- Joseph and Louis Papan (in *Homework 8: To Kearny by Equation)*

- Louis Vieux (in *Homework 8: To Kearny by Equation*)

- George Bent (in *Homework 10: If I Could See This Thing*)

- Biddy Mason (in *Homework 21: Biddy Mason*)

- James P. Beckwourth (in *Homework 27: Catching Up in Auburn*)

When these individuals' names appear in activities, let students know that they are reading about people who actually existed. Tell them, however, that other characters are fictitious.

The Overland Trail

from *Women's Diaries of the Westward Journey*

Between 1840 and 1870, a quarter of a million Americans crossed the continental United States, some twenty-four hundred miles of it, in one of the great migrations of modern times. They went West to claim free land[*] in the Oregon and California Territories, and they went West to strike it rich by mining gold and silver. Men and women knew they were engaged in nothing less than extending American possession of the continent from ocean to ocean....

The westward movement was a major transplanting of young families. All the kinfolk who could be gathered assembled to make that hazardous passage together....

The emigrants came from Missouri, Illinois, Iowa, and Indiana, and some all the way

*Note to students: While the land was offered "free" to these migrants, it was not land that was free for the taking. It was the home of the indigenous peoples who had been living there for thousands of years.

Continued on next page

3. Background Reading: *The Overland Trail*

You might ask various students to read this aloud as the rest of the class follows along.

from New York and New Hampshire. Most of them had moved to "free land" at least once before, and their parents and grandparents before them had similarly made several removals during their lifetime. These were a class of "peasant proprietors." They had owned land before and would own land again. They were young and consumed with boundless confidence, believing the better life tomorrow could be won by the hard work of today....

The journey started in the towns along the Missouri River between St. Joseph and Council Bluffs. These settlements came to be known as the "jumping-off places." In the winter months emigrants gathered to join wagon parties and to wait for the arrival of kin. It was an audacious journey through territory that was virtually unknown. Guidebooks promised that the adventure would take no more than three to four months time—a mere summer's vacation. But the guidebooks were wrong. Often there was no one in a wagon train who really knew what the roads would bring, or if there were any roads at all. Starting when the mud of the roads began to harden in mid-April, the emigrants would discover that the overland passage took every ounce of ingenuity and tenacity they possessed. For many, it would mean six to eight months of grueling travel, in a wagon with no springs, under a canvas that heated up to 110° by midday, through drenching rains and summer storms. It would mean swimming cattle across river and living for months at a time in tents.

From *Women's Diaries of the Westward Journey* by Lillian Schlissel. Copyright © 1983 by Schocken Books Inc. Reprinted by permission of Schocken Books, published by Pantheon Books, a division of Random House, Inc.

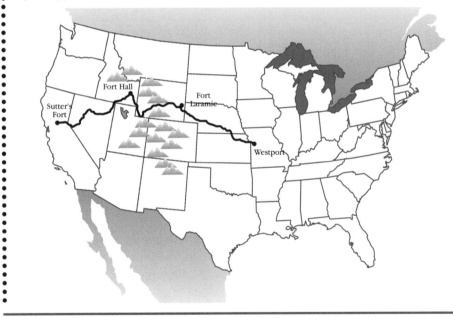

4. Focused Free-Writing

After students view a video or read background material, you can have them do focused free-writing in preparation for a class discussion.

Here are a few topics students can write about.

- What did you learn from the video about the Overland Trail?

- What do you know about this period of time in the history of the United States?

- If you were going back in time from today to that period, what would you bring with you?

After about five minutes, ask for volunteers to share from their writing as a way to summarize or clarify ideas from the video or the readings.

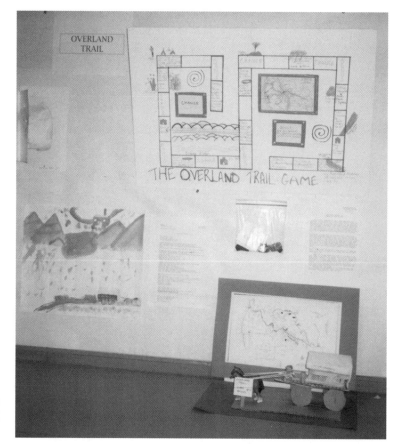

Students in Betty Chiu's class illustrate the Overland Trail in three different ways.

Homework 1

Just Like Today

Throughout history there has been movement of people from place to place.

In this assignment, consider a present-day movement of people and compare it to the movement of people along the Overland Trail.

There are many different levels on which you can consider this topic.

For instance, you can look at your own family and a move they made, or you can look at the movement of people from one country to another.

Write about how the two movements—Overland Trail and present-day—are similar and about how they are different. You might comment on why the people are moving in each case and how they get from one place to another.

Homework 1:
Just Like Today

In tonight's homework assignment, students will consider movements of people in recent times and how they compare to the movement of people in the mid-1800s.

DAY 2 Creating Families

Students begin creating their own Overland Trail families.

Mathematical Topics

- Creating examples that fit a set of constraints
- Interpreting ambiguous problems

Outline of the Day

In Class

1. Discuss *Homework 1: Just Like Today*

2. Have students read *Overland Trail Families*

3. *The Family*
   - Each group of students creates four Overland Trail families
   - Students use *Overland Trail Names* as the source of names for their family members
   - The activity will be completed and discussed on Day 3

4. Introduce *POW 8: The Haybaler Problem*
   - Students use manipulatives to work through a simplified version of the POW

At Home

Homework 2: Hats for the Families

POW 8: The Haybaler Problem
(due Day 8)

Special Materials Needed

- Manipulatives for illustrating *POW 8: The Haybaler Problem*
- Folders in which groups will keep materials about their Overland Trail families

Discuss With Your Colleagues

What Is Mathematics?

Activities like *The Family* and others in this unit (including *POW 10: On Your Own*) do not fall into any traditional category in the high school mathematics curriculum.

Use the brief commentary headed "For teachers: The mathematics of *The Family*" (on page 15) to start a discussion with your colleagues about what the boundaries should be for the subject matter of the mathematics classroom.

1. Discussion of *Homework 1: Just Like Today*

For discussion in groups: "How did the movement you wrote about compare to the Overland Trail movement?"

Ask students to work within their groups and share the comparisons they made of two movements. The spade card students can begin and students can take turns until each member of the group has had a chance to share.

You may also want to ask for a few volunteers to share with the entire class. Student responses may vary so greatly that you will have to play it by ear as to how to help the discussion along.

Point out to students that while the events the class will be studying happened about 150 years ago, many of the issues that were important then are still important now.

2. Background Reading: *Overland Trail Families*
(see facing page)

The following excerpt gives descriptions of actual families that traveled the trail. You can have a student (or students) read it to the class in preparation for groups forming their own Overland Trail families.

IMP coordinator, Donna Gaarder, visits a school and talks with students.

Overland Trail Families

[From the diary of Catherine Haun]

Ada Millington was twelve when her family set out for California. It was a large family; her father, who had five children by his first marriage, was traveling with his second wife and their six children. The youngest was a year and a half old. In addition, there were five young hired hands. And there was Mrs. Millington's sister and brother-in-law, their children, and their hired hands. And there was the brother-in-law's sister, stepfather and mother. The party seemed large and secure. . . .

Our own party consisted of six men and two women. Mr. Haun, my brother Derrick, Mr. Bowen, three young men to act as drivers, a woman cook and myself. . . .

A regulation "prairie schooner" drawn by four oxen and well filled with suitable supplies, with two pack mules following on behind was the equipment of the Kenna family. There were two men, two women, a lad of fifteen years, a daughter thirteen and their half brother six weeks of age. This baby was our mascot and the youngest member of the company. . . .

One family by the name of Lemore consisted of man, wife and two little girls. They had only a large express wagon drawn by four mules and meager but well chosen, supply of food and feed. A tent was strapped to one side of the wagon, a roll of bedding to the other side, baggage, bundles, pots, pans and bags of horse feed hung on behind; the effect was really grotesque. . . .

Mr. West from Peoria, Ill. had another man, his wife, a son Clay about 20 years of age and his daughter, America, eighteen. Unfortunately Mr. West had gone to the extreme of providing himself with such a heavy wagon and load they were deemed objectionable as fellow argonauts. After disposing of some of their supplies they were allowed to join us. . . .

A mule team from Washington, D.C. was very insufficiently provisioned. . . [by] a Southern gentlemen "unused to work. . . ." They deserted the train at Salt Lake as they could not proceed with their equipment. . . .

Much in contrast to these men were four batchelors Messers Wilson, Goodall, Fifield and Martin, who had a wagon drawn by four oxen and two milch cows following behind. The latter gave milk all the way to the sink of the Humboldt where they died, having acted as draught animals for several weeks after the oxen had perished. Many a cup of milk was given to the children of the train and the mothers tried in every way possible to express their gratitude.

3. *The Family*
(see page 16)

The Family describes four types of family units that might have been part of a wagon train. Each group of students will create a family of each type and, during the course of the unit, they will follow the planning and movement of these families along the trail. Keeping track of these families should help to make the setting more vivid to students and should promote students' interest in the unit and in the historical period.

You can begin by having students briefly look over the activity. Tell them that each group will be creating one family of each type.

Emphasize that the group as a whole is responsible for creating the families, even though each student will have final responsibility for one particular family. You may want to let all group members begin together to create the families, and then announce the specific assignment of responsibilities.

Here is one possible scheme for assigning final responsibility for the individual families.

- The club card member should have final responsibility for the *minimal family*.

- The diamond card member should have final responsibility for the *large family*.

- The heart card member should have final responsibility for the *nonfamily*.

- The spade card member should have final responsibility for the *conglomerate family*.

If some groups have other than four members, you will have to adjust accordingly. It is essential that each group create one of each type of family and keep track of them, even if this means some students must keep track of more than one family.

Students will have part of tomorrow's class period to complete the assignment. You may want to bring the class together for discussion partway through the assignment—for example, after all groups have created their "minimal families."

Reminder: Leave about ten minutes at the end of today's class period to introduce *POW 8: The Haybaler Problem*.

• *Constraints*

Point out that each family is subject to a set of conditions, or **constraints**.

There are some ambiguities in the wording of these constraints, such as use of the word *between* in the description of the large family. If students raise these issues, urge them to make decisions as a group about how to treat these ambiguities, but to be aware that they are imposing their own interpretations. They need to develop the initiative to begin making their own sense out of mathematical situations.

> *Note:* The term *constraint* is a useful one in discussing real-life problems. You can use it informally here, perhaps defining it, if necessary, as a "restriction" or "condition." Constraints will play an important role in the Year 2 unit, *Cookies*, in which the term is used frequently.

• *Folders for the families*

Each group should have a folder in which they keep the names of the people in their four family units. The folders should be kept in class so groups can use them even when group members are absent. Students should also have a copy of their group's folder contents for their own use on homework assignments.

The folders should also be used to keep track of the supply information that is discussed in *Planning for the Long Journey* (Days 5 and 6). Subsequent assignments may require students to add to or to change information in their folders.

• *For teachers: The mathematics of "The Family"*

The Family, like many activities in this unit, does not fit into any standard category of mathematics usually associated with high school. But when combined with its companion activity, tonight's *Homework 2: Hats for the Families,* it gives students experience in the important mathematical task of creating examples and counterexamples.

Both in applied situations and in theoretical discussions, mathematical problems often require one to ask such questions as, Is this possible? How might this be set up? What restrictions does this condition create?

The families that students create will appear at various points throughout the unit. The variations from one family to the next will serve as the basis for a set of concrete examples from which students can create general rules.

• *For your convenience: What families should look like*

As you watch students working on *The Family,* you may find it helpful to have a sense of what the size and structure of each Overland Trail family should be. For your convenience, here is a summary of some of the limitations that result from the descriptions. (Students will find these maximum and minimum family sizes in tonight's homework.)

Minimal family. This family will have at least 3 and at most 7 people altogether, with the smallest possible family consisting of a pair of adult siblings and one child.

Large family. In determining the size of the large family we are assuming that "between 1 and 6 hired

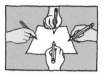

The Family

Your group is going to be responsible for the planning and travel of four family units on the wagon train. In this activity, you will decide on the composition of each of your families.

Here are some general conventions.

- Anyone more than 14 years old is considered an adult.

- A *young child* is anyone less than 6 years old.

- An *older child* is anyone from the age of 6 through the age of 14.

- Only adults have children.

- Hired hands are adults and are not related to the other members of the family unit. They are considered to be part of the family with which they travel.

- A wagon can accommodate at most 6 people. So a family unit of 6 or fewer people needs only one wagon, but a family unit of between 7 and 12 people needs two wagons, a family unit of between 13 and 18 people needs three wagons, and so on.

The information below and on the next two pages describes four types of family units that traveled on the trail. Your group should create one family of each type, and each group member will have final responsibility for one of the families.

Make up a complete list of all the people in each family. *Give each person a first and last name, an age, and a sex.* (Use names from the list in *Overland Trail Names.*)

Record how many adult men, adult women, older children, and young children there are in each family. (You will use this information in later assignments.)

The Minimal Family

Some family units were quite small, by the standards of the time. A *minimal family* fits the conditions listed on the facing page.

Continued on next page

hands" includes the case of just 1, and that children are not married.

The large family will have at least 13 and at most 25 people altogether, with the smallest possible family consisting of six adults and seven children. The six adults could be a married couple (the parents), the married parents of one of them (the grandparents), one great-grandparent, and one hired hand.

Nonfamily. This group will have at least 2 and at most 12 people

- There are more adults than children.

- There is at least one child.

- There are at least as many adult men as adult women.

- There is at most one married couple.

- There is at least one pair of adult siblings.

- The number of people in the family unit is less than eight.

The Large Family

In a large family, one finds not only many children but many other adults in addition to the father and mother. A *large family* meets these criteria.

- The number of children is greater than the number of adults.

- There are between one and six hired hands.

- Four generations of family members are represented.

- At least two married couples are present in the group.

- There are more young children than there are older children.

- There are at most 25 family members.

Continued on next page

altogether, with the smallest possible family consisting of two male adults.

Conglomerate family. This family will have at least 3 and at most 12 people altogether, with the smallest possible family consisting of two partial families, one with just one adult, one with an adult and a young child.

Thus, altogether, the four families created by a group will have anywhere from 21 to 56 people.

The Nonfamily

Some groups traveling on the trail were hardly families at all.
A *nonfamily* is one that fits the conditions below.

- There are no married couples.

- Any adult women in the group are traveling with a brother or a father.

- There is at most one adult woman for each four adult men.

- The number of adult men in the group can range from two to eight.

- There is no more than one child for each five adults.

- There are at least as many older children as young children.

The Conglomerate Family

Sometimes small families banded together into a single unit for the trip. Such a *conglomerate family* meets these conditions.

- There are two or three "partial families" in the unit.

- Each partial family includes at least one adult.

- Each partial family has fewer than five people in it.

- The total number of children equals at least one-third the total number of adults.

- There are more young children than older children.

Overland Trail Names

The names in these lists are taken from sources contemporary to the period of the Overland Trail.

Last Names

Ackley	Cazneau	Frizzell	Kelsey	Smith
Adams	Clappe	Frost	Ketcham	Spencer
Agatz	Clarke	Fulkerth	Knight	Stewart
Allen	Collins	Geer	Mason	Stone
Ashley	Colt	Goltra	Millington	Tabor
Bailey	Cooke	Hall	Minto	Ward
Ballou	Cox	Hanna	Norton	Washburn
Behrins	Dalton	Haun	Parker	Waters
Bell	Deady	Helmick	Parrish	Welch
Belshaw	Duniway	Hines	Pengra	Whitman
Bennett	Findley	Hixon	Porter	Wilson
Bogart	Fish	Hockensmith	Powers	Wood
Brown	Foster	Hodder	Pringle	
Buck	Fowler	Hunt	Rudd	
Butler	French	Jones	Sanford	
Carpenter	Frink	Kellogg	Sawyer	

Female First Names

Abigail	Catherine	Esther	Louise	Nancy
Ada	Celinda	Hallie	Lucinda	Rebecca
Amelia	Charlotte	Helen	Lucy	Roxana
America	Clara	Jane	Lydia	Sarah
Ann	Elizabeth	Julia	Margaret	Susan
Caroline	Ellen	Lavinia	Mary	Velina

Male First Names

Addison	Evan	Henry	Lafayette	Robert
Alpheus	Ezra	Holmes	Lewis	Samuel
Charles	Francis	James	Moses	Solomon
Dexter	George	Jared	Perry	Thomas
Edward	Gilbert	Jay	Peter	Tosten
Enoch	Godfry	John	Richard	William

- *For reference:"Overland Trail Names"*

  Overland Trail Names provides students with a list of settlers' names from the period. They should use names from this list for their family members, since special things happen to family members with specific names in later activities.

4. Introduction of POW 8: The Haybaler Problem

(see next page)

Allow time at the end of the class period to introduce *POW 8: The Haybaler Problem*.

To give students a sense of what's going on in this problem, you might demonstrate a simplified version of it. You can use cubes or other objects to represent the bales of hay. Perhaps do a case with four bales, giving students the weights of the individual bales and having them find the weights in pairs.

"If the individual bales have these weights, what are the weights when they are weighed in pairs?"

For example, if bale 1 weighs 20 kg, bale 2 weighs 26 kg, bale 3 weighs 29 kg, and bale 4 weighs 38 kg, students should be able to see that there are six possible combinations and to find the weight for each pair. (For example, bales 1 and 2 together weigh 46 kg; bales 1 and 3 together weigh 49 kg, and so forth.) They will get six combination weights, and should see that the POW asks them to work backwards, from the combination weights to the weights of the individual bales.

Be sure students understand that each weight given in the POW represents the weight of two bales. You may also want to point out that they don't necessarily know which weight combination corresponds to which pair of bales. Students will need to experiment with numbers and organize their information in new ways in order to solve the problem.

This POW is scheduled for discussion on Day 8.

• •

Groups are bonding together and helping each other—they are playing the roles well—a very good unit to foster cooperation, interdependency, personal responsibility to the group, and "sticking-with-it-until-the-end."

Thom Dodd
IMP teacher

POW 8   *The Haybaler Problem*

The Situation

You have five bales of hay.

For some reason, instead of being weighed individually, they were weighed in all possible combinations of two: bales 1 and 2, bales 1 and 3, bales 1 and 4, bales 1 and 5, bales 2 and 3, bales 2 and 4, and so on.

The weights of each of these combinations were written down and arranged in numerical order, *without keeping track of which weight matched which pair of bales*. The weights in kilograms were 80, 82, 83, 84, 85, 86, 87, 88, 90, and 91.

Your Task

Your initial task is to find out how much each bale weighs. In particular, you should determine if there is more than one possible set of weights, and explain how you know.

Once you are done looking for solutions, look back over the problem to see if you can find some easier or more efficient way to find the weights.

Continued on next page

Write-up

1. *Problem Statement*

2. *Process:* This is especially important in this problem. Include a description of any materials you used. Be sure to discuss ways in which you tried to attack the problem but which didn't lead anywhere.

   Also discuss any insights you had after working on the problem about other ways you might have solved it.

3. *Solution:* Show both how you know your weights work and how you know that you have not missed some other possibilities.

4. *Extensions*

5. *Evaluation*

Adapted from *Problem of the Week* by Lyle Fisher and Bill Medigovich (Dale Seymour Publications, © 1981).

Homework 2   Hats for the Families

Everyone on the westward journey on the Overland Trail will be spending long hours in the hot sun. Before setting out on the road, each person will need to have one good hat to help keep the sun off.

1. What is the minimum and maximum number of hats that might be needed for each type of family unit?

2. What would be the minimum and maximum number of hats that might be needed for a wagon train consisting of one family unit of each type?

3. Estimate the number of hats that might be needed for all the family units in your class. Explain your reasoning.

Homework 2: Hats for the Families

In order to do tonight's homework, students will need to use the descriptions from today's activity, *The Family,* but they do not need to have finished the activity.

Sharing Families

Mathematical Topics

- Finding numbers that fit several conditions
- Compiling data

Outline of the Day

In Class

1. Discuss *Homework 2: Hats for the Families*
   - Identify minimum and maximum possible size for each type of family
2. Complete and discuss *The Family* (from Day 2)
   - Compare family sizes with results from *Homework 2: Hats for the Families*

- Post a chart summarizing the sizes of the families created
- Each student needs to record certain information about the families for use later in the unit

At Home

Homework 3: The Search for Dry Trails

1. Discussion of Homework 2: Hats for the Families

"What were the smallest and the largest sizes you got for each type of family?"

You might give students time to compare answers within their groups while you make note of those who did their homework. Next, you can ask students to report on the minimum and maximum number of members in their family units, perhaps challenging the rest of the class to beat the minimum or maximum numbers presented.

Keep in mind that there may not be clearcut "right answers" for parts of this homework, since a few of the instructions in *The Family,* on which the homework is based, are ambiguous.

"What assumptions did you make?"

However, students should recognize that once these ambiguities are resolved, Questions 1 and 2 of *Homework 2: Hats for the Families* do have specific answers. Encourage students to question one another's answers and find out what assumptions were made that caused one person's answer to differ from another's.

For Question 2, students should see that they must add all the minimum numbers or add all the maximum numbers. This is an intuitive notion and should be kept that way.

Question 3 of the homework involves making estimates as to what the families for the whole class will look like. If these estimates are at all reasonable, then their work should be considered correct. For example, students might use the average of their minimum and maximum numbers as the class average, and should use the number of groups in the class.

2. Completing *The Family*

The groups will spend the rest of the day completing the work of creating their families and looking at the results. (Groups that finish early can work on the POW.)

"How many men, women, and children in each of your families?"

When all groups are done creating their families, compile a list of sizes of the families created, letting heart card students report for their groups. Have groups talk about any assumptions that they needed to make in order to do this activity.

"What assumptions did you make?"

You may wish to organize the information using a chart like this, or you can let the students decide how to organize it.

	Group number							
	1	2	3	4	5	6	7	8
Minimal family								
Large family		[Table entries would show the number of men,						
Nonfamily		women, and children in each of the families.]						
Conglomerate								

Post the chart for reference throughout the unit.

"How many adults are there in all of the class's families combined? How many children?"

For use in later assignments, ask students to find the total number of adults and the total number of children in their entire class wagon train.

The posted chart can be compared with homework results, confirming that no family of a given kind was smaller than the minimum number possible or larger than the maximum number possible (as determined in *Homework 2: Hats for the Families*). Students can also compare their estimates on Question 3 of the homework with the actual results.

Remind students that some of the families may require more than one wagon. (This fact will be needed in *Homework 8: To Kearny by Equation*.)

• *Important: Recording information*

Tell students that the Overland Trail families will be referred to throughout the unit, so students need to keep track of certain information. Specifically, *each student* will need to know

- the number of men, women, and children in each of the four families created by the student's own group

- which family the student is personally responsible for

- the total number of adults and the total number of children in the entire wagon train (which consists of all the individual families created by all the groups)

- the last names of the members of the four families created by the student's own group

You may want to suggest that students make a chart containing this information, similar to the one that was posted.

Serena Pon's classroom is enhanced with posters created by student groups for "The Family."

Homework 3 The Search for Dry Trails

The Setting

Families used to arrive in the Westport area (near present-day Kansas City, Missouri) during the winter before they were to make their journey across the west. Around April, the muddy trails would begin to dry and the settlers would start their trip. But rainy weather could still make roads muddy and significantly slow a wagon train's progress.

Continued on next page

*Homework 3:
The Search for
Dry Trails*

The purpose of tonight's homework assignment is to get students to think about how data can be used and interpreted in context.

• •

The three main trails to the eastern slope of the Rocky Mountains were

- the Smoky Hill Trail, which followed the Smoky Hill River to Denver, Colorado
- the Santa Fe Trail, which followed the Arkansas River to southern Colorado
- the Oregon Trail, which followed the North Platte River to Laramie, Wyoming

Note: These descriptions use the names given by settlers to places and geographical features.

Your Problem

Over the years, the owner of the Westport Trading Post has gotten word back from various friends concerning the rainfall that they encountered on their routes.

The owner has compiled the table below, in which each entry for a given trail represents a different year on that trail.

Santa Fe Trail		Smoky Hill Trail		Oregon Trail	
Name	Number of rainy days	Name	Number of rainy days	Name	Number of rainy days
William	24	Tosten	18	Enoch	42
Amelia	3	Roxana	16	Sarah	9
Ezra	21	Hallie	13	Godfry	11
Lavinia	5	Ada	14	Alpheus	10
Moses	23	Dexter	19	Ann	12
				Jared	13

A big argument occurs one evening. It seems that family members looking at the same data cannot agree on which trail would be the driest. (Of course, the dryness of a trail was not the only factor in choosing the route.)

1. If you were deciding for your Overland Trail family, which trail would you choose? Why?

2. Give good reasons why each of the two paths that you did not choose could have been chosen.

Students do some work on POW 8.

Mathematical Topics

- Calculating the mean
- Using data to make decisions

Outline of the Day

In Class

1. Discuss *Homework 3: The Search for Dry Trails*
   - Focus on the limitations of using the mean as a decision-making tool
2. Provide time for group work on *POW 8: The Haybaler Problem,* with manipulatives available

At Home

Homework 4: Family Constraints

Special Materials Needed

- Manipulatives for working on *POW 8: The Haybaler Problem*

1. Discussion of Homework 3: The Search for Dry Trails

You can ask students to compare ideas in their groups while you check who did the homework.

"Which trail did you choose? Why?"

Next, ask for a show of hands with respect to which trail people would take, and let individuals defend their choices.

There are good reasons for picking each of the trails. Here are a few.

- The Smoky Hill Trail has the most consistent rainfall and therefore is the most predictable.

- The Santa Fe Trail has the lowest mean. Also, it has the driest individual years among all listings in the table.

- If you throw out the first entry, the Oregon Trail has the lowest average of the lot, by a pretty good margin.

The discussion should make clear that the mean is not necessarily the best tool for decision-making (although it played an important role in *The Game of Pig*).

2. Class Time on *POW 8: The Haybaler Problem*

Let students spend some time working on the POW in their groups. Make manipulatives, such as cubes, available for students to use to represent the bales.

Here are some questions you might suggest that groups try to answer if they appear to be getting too frustrated (but not before!).

- How much do the two lightest bales weigh?

- How much do the two heaviest bales weigh?

- Which two bales must be weighed to get the second lightest weighing?

- Can you find the weight of all the bales together?

Remind students that it is especially important to discuss process in their POW write-up, because the actual weights, once found, are not that interesting. They should explain how they know they have all the possible solutions, and should also look for simpler ways to approach the problem and describe the approaches they found.

Homework 4: Family Constraints
(see facing page)

Tonight's homework asks students to analyze information about two families in order to discuss some equations.

The different uses of variables are an important part of this unit. This activity exposes students to the use of a variable as an "unknown" in an equation.

Homework 4   Family Constraints

The families described in the following questions do not necessarily belong to an Overland Trail wagon train.

1. The Hickson household contains three people, of different generations. The total of the ages of the three family members is 90.

   a. Find reasonable ages for the three Hicksons.

   b. Find another reasonable set of ages for them.

Continued on next page

c. One student, in solving this problem, wrote

$$C + (C + 20) + (C + 40) = 90$$

i. What do you think C means here?

ii. How do you think the student got 20 and 40?

iii. What set of ages do you think the student came up with?

2. There are four members in the Jackson family, again representing three generations. As in the Hickson household, the total of the ages of these people is 90.

a. Find a possible set of ages in which there are two children, one parent, and one grandparent.

b. Find a possible set of ages in which there is one child, two parents, and one grandparent.

c. Find a possible set of ages in which there is one child, one parent, and two grandparents.

d. In solving Question 2a, one student wrote

$$C + C + (C + 18) + (C + 36) = 90$$

i. What does C represent here?

ii. What do 18 and 36 represent?

iii. Why do you think this student used 18 and 36 while the student in Question 1c used 20 and 40?

iv. What set of ages do you think this student came up with?

DAY 5 *Planning for the Long Journey*

Students begin planning supplies for their Overland Trail families.

Mathematical Topics

- Using a variable and an equation to represent a problem situation
- Planning and estimation

Outline of the Day

In Class

1. Discuss *Homework 4: Family Constraints*
    - Emphasize the use of an equation to represent information about a problem situation

2. *Planning for the Long Journey*
    - Students brainstorm about what supplies to bring on the journey and decide how much of each item will be needed
    - Discuss Part I as a class and then introduce Part II
    - Part II of the activity will be completed on Day 6

At Home

Homework 5: Lunchtime

---

1. Discussion of *Homework 4: Family Constraints*

Some questions to discuss in groups: "Can you write an equation for someone's solution to Question 1a?"

Students can begin by discussing the homework in their groups, perhaps using some of these suggestions to focus their discussions.

- Take a solution that one person in the group came up with for Question 1a, and write an equation for it similar to the one shown in Question 1c.

*"Did you find a
solution to
Question 2c?"
"Calculate the
average age in the
family for different
solutions to
Question 1. What
do you notice?"*

- Was it possible to come up with a household with two grandparents in Question 2c? Why or why not?

- Calculate the average age of family members for each solution you found for Question 1. What do you notice? Can anyone explain why that happens? What about Question 2?

After students have had time for group discussion, the entire class can hold a discussion to share conclusions and ideas.

The class discussion should include the term **equation** as used in this activity. Question 1c is the first use in the IMP curriculum of a variable in an equation as a means of representing information about an unknown quantity. This use of variables will be developed further over the course of the unit.

2. *Planning for the Long Journey*
(see page 38)

Tell the class that now that they have created their Overland Trail families, they can move on to the next step in getting ready for the journey.

Use the map of the United States to point out once again where they are. The first leg of the journey takes them from Westport, Missouri, to Fort Laramie, Wyoming. Wagon trains traveled about 20 miles each day during this part of the journey.

> In *Planning for the Long Journey,* students will make decisions about what their families should take on the trip. We recommend that students work on Part I and discuss that as a class. They can then move on to Part II.
>
> Part II will be completed tomorrow.

• *Part I*

> Often the early stage of the problem-solving process, including the process of solving mathematics problems, is a kind of "messing around" with materials, ideas, and questions. Part I of the activity (Questions 1 and 2) allows for such a period of brainstorming for the planning process.

Make sure that everyone knows what *brainstorm* means: they are simply to offer suggestions for consideration, and not evaluate or pass judgment on anyone else's suggestions.

*"What supply items
did you decide on?"*

Give groups a chance to brainstorm, and then bring the class together and have the groups report.

You can compile and post a master list of possible supply items on chart paper. Also make note of any questions students raise.

• Part II

You can make a transition from Part I to Part II by commenting on the supply list students have generated, perhaps singling out some ingenious suggestions. Assure students that they have come up with some good ideas, especially if they have items not in *Overland Trail Price List*.

Tell the class that for Part II they will be making their final decisions on certain supplies from a predetermined list of supplies and prices. Have them look at *Overland Trail Price List*. Point out that this is a limited list of supplies—presumably they have other supplies as well that are not included in this purchase activity.

You may want to suggest that the group work together on the purchases for all four of its families, but that each group member is to have the final decision for the Overland Trail family for which he or she is personally responsible.

Note: The amounts of the specified items—gunpowder, sugar, and beans—that groups purchase will affect some activities later on (see especially *Previous Travelers* on Day 15 and *Homework 19: What We Needed*). But it is not important that they select the "right" amounts now.

Visiting teachers observe the interaction among students.

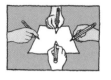

Planning for the Long Journey

Your group will be planning the Overland Trail trip for the four families you created.

The first leg of the journey takes you from Westport, Missouri, to Fort Laramie, Wyoming, some 600 miles away. Wagon trains traveled about 20 miles each day during this part of the journey.

In this activity, you will choose supplies for the first leg of the journey.

Continued on next page

Part I: Generating Ideas

1. The first task is to identify those supplies you think the four Overland Trail families will need. Brainstorm to create a list. Be specific. For example, don't just say *tools*—make a list of the tools that you think it would be important to take. Don't just say *food*—include in your list the different kinds of food the family will need.

2. As you brainstorm and compile this tentative list, questions may occur to you that you cannot answer. *Write these down* to share with the rest of the class.

Part II: Making Decisions

3. *Overland Trail Price List* gives the cost for certain items that you may wish to purchase. Assume that you have $10 for each Overland Trail person to spend on these supplies. Decide how much of each of these items you want to buy for each of your group's Overland Trail families.

   Your purchase list must include gunpowder, sugar, and beans. You may wish to save some money for use along the trail.

   Note: Whatever you purchase now, an identical amount will be ordered to be waiting for you in Fort Laramie when you arrive there. Unless you make changes when you get to Fort Laramie, those will be your supplies from Fort Laramie to the next major stop, Fort Hall. The supplies you purchase may affect the fate of your Overland Trail families on their trip across the country.

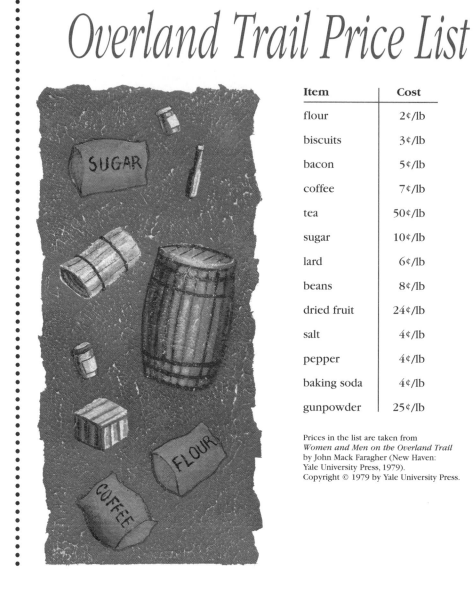

Overland Trail Price List

Item	Cost
flour	2¢/lb
biscuits	3¢/lb
bacon	5¢/lb
coffee	7¢/lb
tea	50¢/lb
sugar	10¢/lb
lard	6¢/lb
beans	8¢/lb
dried fruit	24¢/lb
salt	4¢/lb
pepper	4¢/lb
baking soda	4¢/lb
gunpowder	25¢/lb

Prices in the list are taken from
Women and Men on the Overland Trail
by John Mack Faragher (New Haven:
Yale University Press, 1979).
Copyright © 1979 by Yale University Press.

• *For reference: "Overland Trail Price List"*

Students will use this list in Part II of *Planning for the Long Journey*.

Homework 5   Lunchtime

Imagine that the students in your mathematics class are going to have lunch together. The meal will consist of four parts.

- Main dish
- Side dish
- Dessert
- Beverage

1. Make a list of the items that will have to be purchased.

2. How much of each item will be needed? Explain how you made your decision.

3. Find the cost of each item on the list either by asking a person in your house who shops and would know, or by going to the grocery store and getting the actual price.

4. Compute the total cost of the food for lunch.

5. How much should each student be charged in order for the class to be able to purchase the food? Explain your answer.

Homework 5: Lunchtime

Tonight's assignment is broadly similar to today's classwork, except it takes place in the present day. Some teachers have used student plans from this assignment as the basis for a class party later in the year.

You can encourage students to have someone at home help them plan. Tell them that you expect them to be thorough and accurate.

DAY 6 Shoelaces

Students complete their supply planning.

Mathematical Topics

- Planning and estimation

Outline of the Day

In Class

1. Discuss *Homework 5: Lunchtime*
2. Complete *Planning for the Long Journey* (from Day 5)
   - Groups need to keep their supply lists for use later in the unit

At Home

Homework 6: Shoelaces

- Students will need to know the number of men, women, and children in the Overland Trail family for which they are responsible

1. Discussion of *Homework 5: Lunchtime*

"What were the items on your menu and on your shopping list?"
"Does anyone see anything missing from this list?"

You might ask the diamond card members of a couple of groups to share their menus and shopping lists with the class. Ask the class if they notice any items missing from the list.

"How did you get from the prices of individual items to the total cost?"
"How did you decide how much to charge each person?"

Also ask how students got from the prices of individual items to the total cost, and how they decided how much to charge each person. You can point out that determining the cost per person is another use of the *mean*.

2. Completing Work on *Planning for the Long Journey*

Have groups finish their lists of items to bring on the trip. Groups that finish early can work on their POWs.

Collect the final lists from the groups. The lists should eventually be put into each group's folder for use later in the unit (for example, in *Homework 8: To Kearny by Equation* and in *Previous Travelers* on Day 15).

No further discussion of this activity is needed.

Homework 6: Shoelaces
(see facing page)

> This assignment is an important step in the broad development of the use of variables over the next several days.

Tell students that they will need the description of the Overland Trail family for which they are responsible.

You may want to give transparencies and pens to a few students to write out their descriptions from Question 5. (This will save time in class tomorrow.)

Scene from an IMP classroom — collaborative groups at work

Homework 6   Shoelaces

Shoelaces are one small item that must be taken on the Overland Trail. In this assignment you will consider how much of this commodity is needed.

Assume that shoes already have laces, but that you want to be able to replace each lace once

during the journey. (Also assume that each pair of shoes or boots needs its own laces.)

Here is some detailed information about shoelace requirements that you should use.

- Each man needs to bring two pairs of boots and one pair of shoes.
- Each woman needs to bring one pair of boots and two pairs of shoes.
- Each child needs to have three pairs of boots.
- A shoelace for each adult boot is 48 inches long.
- A shoelace for each adult shoe is 32 inches long.
- A shoelace for each child's boot is 24 inches long.

1. How many inches of shoelace does a woman need?

2. How many inches of shoelace does a man need?

3. How many inches of shoelace does a child need?

4. Find the total length of shoelace needed for the specific Overland Trail family for which you are responsible.

5. Describe in words how you used your answers from Questions 1, 2, and 3 to get your answer to Question 4.

Days 7-10

Setting Out with Variables

You've formed your Overland Trail families, packed up some supplies, and off you go from Westport, Missouri, toward Fort Laramie, Wyoming. You're about to see how equations and algebraic expressions may have helped the settlers plan their journey and meet its challenges.

The new POW coming up, *POW 9: Around the Horn,* involves a different journey, with some complicated comings and goings.

This page in the student book introduces Days 7 through 10.

In order to focus on the meaning of variables, students are creating their own "ox expressions" to share with the class.

210

Interactive Mathematics Program

DAY 7 · *The General Shoelace*

Students use variables to express general formulas, and they begin formal work with algebraic expressions and substitution.

Mathematical Topics

- Developing numerical algorithms
- Expressing algorithms in words and symbols
- Review of algebraic notation, such as juxtaposing variables and coefficients
- Substitution in algebraic expressions

Outline of the Day

In Class

1. Select presenters for tomorrow's discussion of *POW 8: The Haybaler Problem*
2. Discuss *Homework 6: Shoelaces*
   - Use descriptions from Question 5 to develop an algebraic expression for the amount of shoelace needed
   - Introduce the term **algebraic expression**
3. Discuss **substitution** and **evaluation**

At Home

Homework 7: Laced Travelers

1. POW Presentation Preparation

Choose three students to make presentations of *POW 8: The Haybaler Problem* tomorrow, and give them pens and overhead transparencies to take home to use in their preparations.

"What should be in your presentation besides your numerical answers?"

Remind them that their presentations should consist of more than just a list of weights. They should look at the write-up instructions for the POW if they need ideas of what to talk about.

Note: Be sure that all students get a turn at giving POW presentations. If you have students who have not yet given one, assign these students before having others make a second POW presentation. Preparing and giving these presentations is an important experience for students.

2. Discussion of Homework 6: Shoelaces

• *Questions 1 through 3*

Ask students to compare results on Questions 1 through 3 in their groups, to be sure that they are using the same values when they move on to discuss Question 4.

For your convenience: A woman needs 224 inches of shoelace; a man needs 256 inches; and a child needs 144 inches.

• *Questions 4 and 5*

"How much shoelace did your Overland Trail family need?"

"Describe in words how you got your answer to Question 4."

Then bring the class together, and have two or three club card students present their work on Question 4. (Since each student is discussing a different Overland Trail family, the numerical answers will be different.)

Question 5 is really the heart of the activity, because it leads to the generalization into variables. You may want to ask several volunteers to read the descriptions they wrote on how they found the answer to Question 4. It's useful to ask for more than one description, even if the descriptions reflect the same arithmetic process.

You will probably get descriptions like this:

"Multiply the number of women by 224, the number of men by 256, and the number of children by 144, and then add these products."

• *Generalizing to variables*

"How can you abbreviate these verbal descriptions by using variables?"

Ask the class how they can abbreviate these verbal descriptions by using variables. If necessary, remind them of the ways they have used variables in In-Out tables or of the way the letter *C* was used in *Homework 4: Family Constraints.*

Insist that they give clear definitions for the letters they introduce. For example, they should say something like, "*W* represents the number of women in the family," instead of "*W* equals women."

The class should be able to come up with an expression like

$$224W + 256M + 144C$$

for the amount of shoelace needed for a family with *W* women, *M* men, and *C* children.

Refer to this combination of numbers and letters as an **algebraic expression**. If needed, review the term *coefficient* and the omission of the multiplication sign in expressions like 224*W*.

You may want to tell students that by convention, we don't normally write *W*224, but that it is acceptable to write *W* • 224.

Be sure students understand that these abbreviations are simply *notational conventions*—that is, agreements among mathematicians that they will write things a certain way. There is nothing inherently wrong about using a multiplication sign between a number and a variable or about placing the variable in front of the coefficient—we just don't usually do it that way. You may want to remind them of their past work with order of operations as another example of mathematical convention.

3. Substitution and Evaluation

"How can you use the expression 224W + 256M + 144C to find the amount of shoelace needed for a family with four women, six men, and five children?"

Provide some examples to illustrate how a general algebraic expression is used to deal with a particular case. For example, ask students to use the expression 224*W* + 256*M* + 144*C* to find the amount of shoelace needed for a family with four women, six men, and five children.

In the discussion, bring out that once an expression such as 224*W* + 256*M* + 144*C* has been developed, the process becomes quite mechanical. It is often helpful to identify two stages in the process.

- *Replacing a variable by the desired numerical value.* In the example above, this means writing out the expression

$$224 • 4 + 256 • 6 + 144 • 5$$

  (Be sure students realize that they need to restore the multiplication signs that were omitted when letters were used.)

- *Carrying out the indicated arithmetic.* This means, for example, finding that the numerical expression 224 • 4 + 256 • 6 + 144 • 5 is equal to 3152.

Many students find it very helpful to carry out the process in these two stages, so that they see the way in which the numbers replace the letters. Isolating the substitution stage is also helpful in finding careless errors.

Note: These two stages are sometimes called **substitution** and **evaluation** respectively, although either term can refer to the overall process. You can use these terms informally, although they are not used in the student materials for this unit. The terminology will be formally introduced in the Year 2 unit *Solve It!*

• *The complete generalization*

"What algebraic expression gives the total amount needed in terms of how much shoelace each woman, man, and child needs?"

Ask students to imagine now that the shoelace requirements for the different categories of people may be changing, and that they want to create an algebraic expression that can be used more generally, once they find out how much shoelace each woman, man, and child needs.

You may want to suggest the use of subscripted variables such as S_W, S_M, and S_C for these amounts.

Note: Students may have seen the use of subscripts in *The Game of Pig*, but you will probably need to review this with them.

Subscript notation is not used in the student materials for this unit except in the supplementary problem *Classroom Expressions,* where the notation is explained. You may prefer to use variables without subscripts at this point.

Basing their work on these new variables, students should develop a single expression for the shoelace requirements of a family, such as

$$WS_W + MS_M + CS_C$$

If needed, point out that we omit the multiplication sign between variables just as we do between a coefficient and a variable.

If time allows, work through some examples of substitution and evaluation for this more complex expression.

Homework 7

Laced Travelers

In *Homework 6: Shoelaces,* you used certain information to find out how much shoelace each man, woman, and child needs.

In this assignment, you are told how much they each need. These amounts are different from those in the previous assignment, and you should use these new amounts to answer the questions below. Suppose that the statements below were true in 1852.

- You could purchase shoelaces for about 2¢ per yard.
- An average wagon train consisted of 25 families.
- An average family had six people in it (counting unmarried relatives and hired hands): two men, one woman, and three children.
- Approximately 150 wagon trains went through Westport, Missouri, in the year 1852 on their way west.
- Each man needed 5 yards of shoelace.
- Each woman needed 4 yards of shoelace.
- Each child needed 3 yards of shoelace.

Continued on next page

Homework 7: Laced Travelers

Be sure that students understand that they should use the data in this homework, and not the results that they found in *Homework 6: Shoelaces.*

You may want to clarify that in the homework, the word "average" is used in the sense of *mean.* For example, the second bulleted item signifies that

• •

Answer these questions.

1. How many yards of shoelace did the settlers who went through Westport in 1852 need altogether?

   Once you've found an answer, describe in words how you did the computation.

2. Write two more interesting questions related to the journey that you can answer from the given data.

3. Answer one of the questions you made up in Question 2.

4. Suppose that in 1853, smaller families were migrating west, so that the mean family size was only five people (one less child). Answer Question 1 for the year 1853 (assuming that the other information is unchanged).

---

25 was the mean number of families per wagon train. (A phrase like "average wagon train" could also be used in the sense of "typical," and would refer to the mode rather than the mean. You may prefer to mention this point in the homework discussion tomorrow.)

POW 8 Presentations

Mathematical Topics

- Continued work expressing algorithms algebraically
- Experimenting with numbers to solve a problem

Outline of the Day

In Class

1. Discuss *Homework 7: Laced Travelers*
   - Continue work on representing computational patterns algebraically
2. Presentations of *POW 8: The Haybaler Problem*
   - Look for a variety of methods to solve the problem
   - Raise the question of whether the solution is unique (even if students can't prove that it is)
3. Introduce *POW 9: Around the Horn*

- Help students see that they may need to make some assumptions

At Home

Homework 8: To Kearny by Equation
- Students will need to know the number of men, women, and children in each of their group's four Overland Trail families

POW 9: Around the Horn (due Day 14)

1. Discussion of Homework 7: Laced Travelers

As students enter, you can have them share questions that they made up for Question 2, and try to answer each other's questions. Meanwhile, ask two or three spade card students to put their word descriptions from Question 1 on overhead transparencies.

"Describe in words how you found the answer."

The main focus of the class discussion should be Question 1 and students' descriptions in words of how they found the answer.

The goal in the discussion is to turn those descriptions into algebraic expressions. (Some students may have already done so.)

For example, suppose one student's description begins

> "You take the 150 wagon trains times the 25 families per train times the length of shoelace per family. The amount per family is twice the amount per man plus the amount per woman plus three times the amount per child. . . ."

"How can you rewrite this sentence without reference to specific numbers?"

Ask students to rewrite this sentence without reference to *specific* numbers. For example, the first sentence would come out something like this.

> "Multiply the number of wagon trains times the number of families per train times the length of shoelace per family."

"How can you use variables to rewrite this sentence as an algebraic expression?"

Finally, ask students to come up with a letter for each quantity in the sentence and to rewrite the sentence as an algebraic expression. For the sentence above, they might let T represent the number of wagon trains, F the number of families per wagon train, and S the total amount of shoelace needed per family.

With those variables, they would represent the total amount of shoelace needed for the entire year by something like TFS.

You should emphasize the difference between an object and the number of such objects, and that it is important to be precise about what a letter represents. For instance, in the example above, F does not represent a family, or the number of people in a family, but represents *the number of families in a wagon train*.

• *Using a more complex expression for S*

"How can you use yesterday's expression (for the amount of shoelace for a single family) in this problem?"

You might ask students to recall the expression they came up with yesterday for the amount of shoelace for a single family, and then ask how they can use that in connection with the expression TFS.

The goal of these questions is to have students replace S with $WS_W + MS_M + CS_C$, giving the combined expression

$$TF(WS_W + MS_M + CS_C)$$

for the total amount of shoelace needed.

• *Continued work with substitution and algebraic expressions*

You may want to provide more examples in which computational procedures are represented by algebraic expressions, although students will have many more opportunities to do such work later in this unit and in other units. Try to include examples with coefficients for the variables as well as expressions in which the variables are only added and multiplied.

"What is the value of TF if there are four wagon trains and five families in each?"

You can also work through some examples going the other way, in which students start with a given, meaningful algebraic expression that uses specific values. For example, you might ask,

> *Suppose there are four wagon trains and five families in each? What is the value of TF and what does it represent?*

If students say that the answer is "4 • 5," you can tell them that it is conventional to express numbers in their simplest, "standard" form (in this case, 20), and that is usually the form that is expected when they are asked to "evaluate" or "find the value of" an expression. In other words, we express the entire process by a statement such as

> "When *T* equals 4 and *F* equals 5, the value of *TF* is 20."

"What does this number 20 represent?"

Be sure to get students to say what the number 20 represents—that is, the total number of families. Tomorrow's activity, *Ox Expressions,* will focus on giving meaning to algebraic questions, and today's examples will help prepare students for it.

"If T equals 4 and F equals 5, then isn't TF equal to 45?"

Some students might think that *TF* has the value 45 when *T* equals 4 and *F* equals 5. Be sure to work through enough examples to free them of this misconception. Again, remind them that it is a mathematical convention that the juxtaposition of variables—putting them next to each other—means multiplication.

2. Presentations of *POW 8: The Haybaler Problem*

Have the three students make their presentations. If they all found the same answer, the presentations can focus on more complex issues, such as the uniqueness of the solution and a search for other methods of approaching the problem.

"If you didn't find another solution, does that prove that there isn't another one?"

Although you might not have any students who were able to prove the uniqueness of the solution, be sure that they recognize the distinction between not being able to find another solution and proving that there are no others.

"Did you assume that the weights were whole numbers? How did that affect your work?"

You can ask if students assumed that the weights of the bales had to be whole numbers, and if so, how that affected their work.

One of the supplemental problems for this unit, *More Bales of Hay,* gives students similar questions to consider. In particular, they are asked to think about whether such problems always have unique answers and in which cases the answers are whole numbers.

Comment: If the combination weights given in *POW 8: The Haybaler*

Problem are thought of as rounded off to the nearest whole number— that is, they are not necessarily exact sums—then there are many solutions, including some that are significantly different from the solution one gets by assuming the combination weights are exact. Our thanks to a student for pointing this out!

3. Introduction of *POW 9: Around the Horn*

(see facing page)

Have students read *POW 9: Around the Horn* and give them some class time to begin working on it.

The problem may seem simple at first, but it requires careful reading. Students may find that acting it out is the best strategy.

Questions will probably arise about whether or not to count a ship that arrives in New York as your ship leaves, or to count a ship that leaves San Francisco as yours arrives there. The issue of the time difference between New York and San Francisco may also need clarification.

The manner in which these questions are resolved is not as important as having students recognize the need for some decisions of interpretation, and having them learn to clarify their assumptions. Emphasize that they need to make their assumptions clear in their write-ups.

This POW is scheduled to be discussed on Day 14.

POW 9   *Around the Horn*

Instead of going overland to reach California, some families migrated west by taking a ship that went around Cape Horn at the tip of South America.

Suppose a ship leaves New York for San Francisco on the first of every month at noon, and at the same instant a ship leaves San Francisco for New York.

Suppose also that each ship arrives exactly six months after it leaves.

If you were on a ship leaving from New York, how many ships from San Francisco would you meet?

Write-up

1. *Problem statement:* If there were any assumptions that you needed to make in order to do this problem, be sure to state them clearly.

2. *Process:* Include any diagrams or materials you used in working on this problem.

3. *Solution*

4. *Extensions*

5. *Evaluation:* Instead of evaluating the problem itself, write an evaluation of your own work on this problem. How well do you think you understood the problem and explained your thinking?

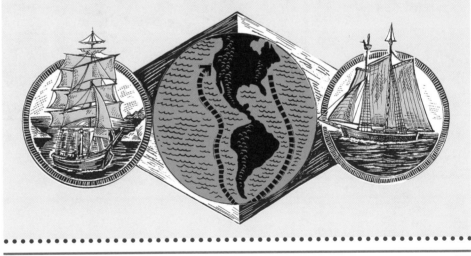

Homework 8 To Kearny by Equation

When the first emigrants went west, crossing rivers was dangerous and time consuming. Travelers were grateful and travel time was shortened when people started ferries to shuttle wagons across the rivers.

The first major stop along the way from Westport to Fort Laramie was at Fort Kearny (now Kearney, Nebraska).

1. Joseph and Lewis Papan, two brothers, were among the "mixed bloods" of the time—those who had one Native American parent and one parent of European origin. They operated a ferry over the Kansas River at Topeka, on the way from Westport to Fort Kearny.

   Make the following assumptions:

   • The fee for crossing the 230-yard-wide river was $1 for each wagon.

   • The ferry captain received pay of 40¢ per hour from the Papans for the time he spent going back and forth.

Continued on next page

Homework 8: To Kearny by Equation

Tonight's homework uses the Overland Trail as the historical context for more work with substitution. You should tell students that they will need information about their group's four families for the assignment.

The Papan brothers could then calculate the profit each of them made by using the equation

$$\text{profit} = \frac{W - 0.4H}{2}$$

in which W was the number of wagons that crossed the river and H was the number of hours that the ferry captain spent going back and forth. (This profit formula takes into account the captain's salary, but does not take into account the Papans' other expenses, such as upkeep of the boat.)

a. Explain why this formula makes sense.

Suppose further that a round trip on the ferry took 20 minutes and that the ferry carried only one family at a time.

b. How much profit would each of the Papan brothers make from the family unit for which you are responsible? (*Reminder:* A family unit of between 7 and 12 people requires two wagons, a family unit of between 13 and 18 people requires three wagons, and so on.)

c. How much profit would each of the Papan brothers make from your group's four family units?

2. Louis Vieux was a business manager, interpreter, and chief of the Potawatomi. He made many trips to Washington to consult with officials about the affairs of Native Americans.

Vieux was also a ferry operator. He operated a ferry and toll bridge over the Vermillion River, the third major river crossing in Kansas.

Suppose that he charged a certain amount for each wagon and then an additional amount for each person, with different amounts for men, women, and children. More specifically, suppose that the amount Louis Vieux charged was given by the equation

$$\text{price to cross (in dollars)} = 0.5W + 0.25M + 0.1F + 0.05C$$

in which W was the number of wagons, M the number of men, F the number of women, and C the number of children.

a. Use this formula to explain what Vieux charged in each of the individual cost categories (that is, for each wagon, for each man, and so forth).

b. What would be the crossing cost for the family unit for which you are responsible?

c. What would be the total cost for your group's four family units?

Interactive Mathematics Program

215

Note: In tomorrow's discussion, students will learn what the consequences are if they did not bring enough cash to cover the tolls in Question 2c.

DAY 9 Ox Expressions

Students explore the use of algebraic expressions in a problem context.

Mathematical Topics

- Developing meaningful algebraic expressions
- Interpreting algebraic expressions using summary phrases

Outline of the Day

In Class

1. Discuss *Homework 8: To Kearny by Equation*
   - Have students make appropriate adjustments in their supply lists
2. *Ox Expressions*
   - Students use specified variables to create meaningful algebraic expressions

- The activity will be discussed on Day 10

At Home

Homework 9: Ox Expressions at Home

Discuss With Your Colleagues

Continuing the Introduction of Variables

As in *Patterns*, this unit focuses on the meaning of variables rather than on their manipulation as algebraic symbols.

The National Council of Teachers of Mathematics *Standards* talks about the need for increased attention at the middle school level to "developing an understanding of variables, expressions, and equations."

Discuss whether that has happened yet at your feeder schools. Are students coming into ninth grade with a sense of what variables, algebraic expressions, and equations are all about?

If so, then you may be able to move quickly through this material. If not, then this stage of the unit forms a crucial part of the foundation of students' mathematical understanding.

1. Discussion of *Homework 8: To Kearny by Equation*

Since each individual and each group will have different answers, you may want to just let the groups go over their answers, rather than have a discussion involving the entire class.

As you circulate among the groups, you can be on the lookout for common sources of confusion that may warrant a discussion with the class as a whole.

Disagreements about the numerical answers may come from at least two sources:

- incorrect values substituted for the individual variables—for example, students may have forgotten to account for some families having more than one wagon

- mistakes in arithmetic, possibly due to misuse of order-of-operations rules

• *Supplies and livestock update*

Each group needs to check if they kept enough cash, when they did *Planning for the Long Journey,* to pay for their tolls from Question 2c of last night's homework.

Tell them that, if not, then their families had to find a shallow place to cross the river with their animals and wagons; unfortunately, in the process, an ox got stuck in the mud and drowned. Also, a 10-pound sack of beans fell from the wagon and was lost in the river.

Groups that did not bring enough cash will need to adjust the information in their folders, crossing 10 pounds of beans off their supply list. (There's no specific action they need to take concerning the lost ox.)

2. Ox Expressions
(see page 64)

Yesterday in class, students created algebraic expressions to describe calculation procedures. Now they will move in the other direction, taking algebraic expressions and interpreting them in terms of the concepts that the variables represent.

Today's main activity, *Ox Expressions,* asks students to come up with as many different meaningful algebraic expressions as possible for a given set of variables. The key idea is to give contextual meaning to algebraic expressions, and not to see them simply as descriptions of a set of arithmetic operations.

Discussion of this activity is scheduled for tomorrow, although you may decide to begin the discussion today. You may want to collect students' write-ups of this activity to get a sense of how well they understand the use of variables to represent parts of a problem situation.

Ask students to briefly look over the activity. You can clarify the activity by reviewing some of yesterday's examples, such as the use of *TF* to represent the total number of families.

"What is a summary phrase for the expression FC?"

You should discuss the idea of a **summary phrase** for meaningful expressions. Emphasize that these phrases should be as concise as possible. For instance, in the example given in the activity, the summary phrase for the expression *FC* is *the number of children in a wagon train*, rather than *the number of families in a wagon train times the number of children in a family*.

If students seem overwhelmed after working a bit on the task, you can ask them to begin by considering just three symbols.

- *M:* the number of **M**en in a family

- *W:* the number of **W**omen in a family

- *C:* the number of **C**hildren in a family

"What does M + W + C represent in terms of the problem?"

Ask the class what the expression $M + W + C$ represents in terms of the problem. They should see that it gives the total number of people in a family. Similarly, you can ask about the expression $M + W$, which represents the number of adults.

"What questions can you express using these variables?"

You can then introduce other variables, such as *F*, *B*, and *D*. The entire class can brainstorm to come up with questions that use those variables, such as "How much water will the women in the wagon train drink altogether on the trip?"

Note: One error students seem to persist in making is to forget to say "number of" in defining variables. For example, they say "*F* is the families in a wagon train" rather than "*F* is the number of families in a wagon train." This is a hard habit to break—you may want to pay attention to it.

Ox Expressions

The table below defines some symbols as variables to represent certain quantities. For example, *F* stands for "the number of **F**amilies in a wagon train." (The **boldface** letters in the table will help to remind you of what each symbol represents.)

A specific numerical value is provided for each variable. You should treat this value as constant for all cases. For example, assume that *every* wagon train contains 25 families. (Of course, these values will probably not be the actual numbers in your class wagon train.)

Symbol	Meaning	Numerical value
F	the number of **F**amilies in a wagon train	25 families per train
M	the number of **M**en in a family	2 men per family
W	the number of **W**omen in a family	1 woman per family
C	the number of **C**hildren in a family	3 children per family
V	the number of wagons (**V**ehicles) per family	1 wagon per family
T	the number of wagon **T**rains in one year	150 trains per year
Y	the number of pairs (**Y**okes) of oxen per wagon	3 yokes per wagon
A	the number of oxen (**A**nimals) per yoke	2 oxen per yoke
P	the weight of one ox (in **P**ounds)	1200 pounds per ox
L	the **L**oad for one wagon (in pounds)	2500 pounds per wagon
G	the amount of **G**rass eaten by one ox in one day (in pounds)	40 pounds of grass per ox per day
H	the amount of water (**H**$_2$O) consumed by one ox in one day (in gallons)	2 gallons of water per ox per day
B	the amount of water (**B**everage) consumed by one person in one day (in gallons)	0.5 gallons of water per person per day
D	the number of **D**ays on the trail	169 days

Using the given letters, it is possible to write many different algebraic expressions. Although you can always substitute numbers for the letters and do the arithmetic, most of the expressions you create will have no real meaning.

Continued on next page

For example, for the expression *MG*, you can multiply the number of men per family by the amount of grass an ox can eat in a day, but the product you get doesn't have any useful application. In other words, *MG* doesn't really mean anything.

But some expressions *do* have a meaning. For example, *FC*, the number of families in a wagon train times the number of children in a family, represents the total number of children traveling in a wagon train. So the expression *FC* has meaning.

The phrase "the number of children traveling in the train" is a concise way to describe the number represented by *FC*. We will call this the **summary phrase.**

The table tells you that there are 25 families in a wagon train, so $F = 25$, and that there are 3 children in a family, so $C = 3$. Therefore, $FC = 25 \cdot 3 = 75$, and there are 75 children in a wagon train. Even if the numbers were different, *FC* would still represent the number of children in a wagon train.

Your Task

Your task is to come up with as many meaningful algebraic expressions as you can, using the symbols above. For each expression, go through the steps listed below.

- Write the expression.

- Explain what the expression means, using a summary phrase.

- Give the numerical value of the expression, based on the values of the individual variables given in the table.

• •

Homework 9 Ox Expressions at Home

In this assignment you continue to work with algebraic expressions and summary phrases.

You will be given specific algebraic expressions and asked to write summary phrases for them; you also will be given specific summary phrases and asked to write algebraic expressions for them.

Reminder: The summary phrase for *FC* is "the number of children on the wagon train" and not "the number of families in a wagon train times the number of children in a family."

The symbols below are the same as those used in *Ox Expressions*. Though no specific numerical values are assigned here, you should assume that each symbol represents a single number.

Symbol	Meaning
F	the number of **F**amilies in a wagon train
M	the number of **M**en in a family
W	the number of **W**omen in a family
C	the number of **C**hildren in a family
V	the number of wagons (**V**ehicles) per family
T	the number of wagon **T**rains in one year
Y	the number of pairs (**Y**okes) of oxen per wagon
A	the number of oxen (**A**nimals) per yoke
P	the weight of one ox (in **P**ounds)
L	the **L**oad for one wagon (in pounds)
G	the amount of **G**rass eaten by one ox in one day (in pounds)
H	the amount of water (**H**$_2$O) consumed by one ox in one day (in gallons)
B	the amount of water (**B**everage) consumed by one person in one day (in gallons)
D	the number of **D**ays on the trail

1. Write a summary phrase for the expression $W + M + C$.

2. Write an algebraic expression for the water consumed in a day by a family.

3. Write a summary phrase for the expression $D(H + B)$.

Continued on next page

Homework 9:
Ox Expressions at Home

Tonight's homework is similar to the class activity, but is more structured. Students should be able to work on it even though they have not yet discussed *Ox Expressions*.

4. Write an algebraic expression for the number of people in a wagon train.

5. Write a summary phrase for the expression *FM*.

6. Write an algebraic expression for the amount of water consumed by an ox on the trip.

7. Does the expression *WL* have a meaning? If so, what is it?

8. Make up a meaningful algebraic expression of your own and give a summary phrase for it.

Sharing Ox Expressions

Students continue to create and interpret algebraic expressions.

Mathematical Topics

- Developing meaningful algebraic expressions
- Interpreting algebraic expressions and writing summary phrases

Outline of the Day

In Class

1. Discuss *Ox Expressions* (from Day 9)
   - Have groups share expressions they made up and give the corresponding summary phrases
   - Encourage other groups to challenge or to improve upon the summary phrases
   - Look for frequently used groups of letters

2. Discuss *Homework 9: Ox Expressions at Home*

- Use the discussion as needed to reinforce ideas that were brought up in the discussion of *Ox Expressions*

At Home

Homework 10: If I Could See This Thing

- Students will need to know the number of adults and children in the entire class wagon train

We suggest that you begin class with a discussion of yesterday's open-ended activity, *Ox Expressions,* rather than with a discussion of *Homework 9: Ox Expressions at Home.* You can choose to spend time on the homework as needed, after seeing how the discussion of *Ox Expressions* goes.

The Social Issues in *The Overland Trail*

This unit touches upon the social history of the period, including the treatment of Native Americans and the often-ignored role of African Americans in the history of the American West. Students also must confront the issue of death on the trail in at least two points in the unit.

These social issues may not be part of your training as a mathematics teacher. How do you and your colleagues approach this material?

1. Discussion of *Ox Expressions*

Note: You may want to give students a bit more time to work on this activity, so they can use insights they got from last night's homework.

Bring the students together to create a class list of meaningful "Ox expressions."

"What's one of your expressions, and what's the summary phrase that goes with it?"

One format that you can use is to go around the class from one group to the next, asking each group to give one of its expressions, together with a summary phrase. Other groups can then challenge the meaningfulness of the phrase or propose an improvement.

You may want to make several complete rounds of the groups before cutting off the discussion.

"Which groups of letters appear frequently?"
"What makes an expression meaningful?"
"Do you think you found all the meaningful expressions?"

Here are some questions you may want to discuss after getting a long list of expressions.

- Which groups of letters do you find appearing frequently? Why is that?

- What determines whether an expression is going to have meaning or not?

- Do you think you found all the meaningful expressions? Why or why not?

2. Discussion of *Homework 9: Ox Expressions at Home*

The discussion of the homework assignment will depend on what happened in the earlier discussion of yesterday's activity, *Ox Expressions*.

If you think a discussion of the homework is needed, you may want to use it as an opportunity to bring out that there may be more than one correct answer to a given problem, for both the algebraic expressions and the summary phrases. For example, if you get both $B(W + M + C)$ and $BW + BM + BC$ for Question 2, you can ask students how these could both be correct. (The distributive property will be treated more formally in the Year 2 unit *Solve It!*)

Note: There are two supplemental activities, *Classroom Expressions* and *Variables of Your Own,* that you can use if you feel that your students need more work relating variables to their meaning and creating good summary phrases. You might want to use them later in the unit rather than as an immediate follow-up to today's work.

Homework 10: *If I Could See This Thing*
(see next page)

The topic of this assignment is gruesome, but it is a fact that people died on the Overland Trail. Take some time to show the class the part of the trail to which this assignment refers—from Fort Kearny, Nebraska, to Fort Laramie, Wyoming, along the North Platte River.

Important: Tell students that for this assignment they need to know the total number of adults and the total number of children in the class wagon train for Question 2a. They should have this information from their work on Day 3.

Homework 10 If I Could See This Thing

No nation was safe from the ravages of smallpox, cholera, measles, scarlet fever, influenza, and tuberculosis. These diseases, which were imported from Europe, took a great toll on Native Americans, bringing death, destruction, and untold misery, killing more people than warfare, slavery, or starvation.

The passage below is taken from a description by George Bent of the Southern Cheyenne nation.

> In '49, the emigrants brought cholera up the Platte Valley, and from the emigrant trains it spread to the Indian camps. "Cramps" the Indians called it....On the Platte whole camps could be seen deserted with tepees full of dead bodies...Our Tribe suffered very heavy loss; half of the tribe died, some old people say.
>
> My Grandmother took the children that summer...to the Canadian [to get] medicine. During the medicine dance an Osage visitor fell down in the crowd with cholera cramps. The Indians broke camp at once and fled in every

Continued on next page

direction. Here a brave man…mounted his horse…and rode through camp could see this thing, if I knew where it was, I would go there and kill it." He was taken with cramps as he rode.

From *Life of George Bent* by Savoie Lotinville (Norman, OK: University of Oklahoma Press, 1968).

1. It has been estimated that between 1492 and 1900 the Native American population decreased by about 90%.

   Use variables and an equation to show how you would find the population of Native Americans at the end of this time period if you knew the population of Native Americans at the beginning of this period.

   Suggestion: Pick a number that you think might represent the population in 1492, and figure out what the 1900 population would have been. Then describe your computation in words, before putting the relationship into equation form using variables.

2. Death occurred among travelers on the Overland Trail as well.

   The fatality rate differed from one wagon train to the next. Assume that in your wagon train, five percent of the adults and ten percent of the children will die of cholera on the road from Fort Kearny, Nebraska, to Fort Laramie, Wyoming.

   a. Figure out how this will change the size of your total class wagon train.

   b. Put the result from Question 2a into an In-Out table in which there are two inputs—the number of adults and the number of children—and the output is the total number of people who will be left in a wagon train after this leg of the journey.

      Add two more rows to this table, using your own choice of values for the two inputs in each row. That is, make up two possible combinations for the number of adults and number of children, and then find the output in your table for each combination.

   c. Introduce variables and write a rule for the In-Out table in Question 2b.

**Days
11-14**

The Graph Tells a Story

They say that a picture is worth a thousand words. While you rest in Fort Laramie and prepare for the next leg of your journey, you look at some posters describing certain aspects of the journey. These posters contain graphs, which depict how two quantities are related. As you will see, graphs are closely related to equations and In-Out tables.

This page in the student book introduces Days 11 through 14.

By the way, your next POW involves a different kind of adventure. In *POW 10: On Your Own,* you will imagine you have finished high school and are living on your own. Are you ready for that?

Teachers preparing to teach "The Overland Trail" get their own presentations ready on "Wagon Train Sketches and Situations."

222

DAY 11

Wagon Train Sketches and Situations

Students use their intuition to determine the meaning of graphs.

Mathematical Topics

- Intuitive interpretation of graphs
- Discrete and continuous graphs
- Dependent and independent variables

Outline of the Day

In Class

1. Remind students to be working on *POW 9: Around the Horn* and get a report on their progress
2. Discuss *Homework 10: If I Could See This Thing*
   - Use numerical examples to clarify use of variables
   - Calculate loss of life for Overland Trail families (from Question 2)
3. *Wagon Train Sketches and Situations*
   - Students interpret graph sketches in terms of the situations they represent and create graph sketches for other situations
4. Discuss *Wagon Train Sketches and Situations*
   - Have students share their interpretations of details in the graphs
   - Introduce the terms **discrete graph** and **continuous graph**
5. Introduce the terms **independent variable** and **dependent variable**

At Home

Homework 11: Graph Sketches

Special Materials Needed

- (Optional) Index cards for use with *Homework 11: Graph Sketches*

1. Reminder on *POW 9: Around the Horn*

"Are you making progress on your POW?"

Although students should have started work on this POW when it was assigned on Day 8, it's probably prudent to take a moment to remind them they should be working on it. You may want to get a sense of how much progress students have made so far, and to remind them of the importance of stating their assumptions in their write-ups.

2. Discussion of *Homework 10: If I Could See This Thing*

Give students time to share their ideas about the homework within their groups. Then have one or two heart card students present results for each problem.

"What did you do to come up with an equation for Question 1?"

You can begin by having two or three students describe exactly what they did on Question 1. Have them talk about the process by which they arrived at an equation, and not just give the equation itself.

Although the computations are simple, the process of introducing and using variables is difficult for many students. The use of variables and equations to represent information about real-world situations is a fundamental idea in mathematics, and you should handle students' confusion with great care, allowing ample time for questions and discussion.

The instructions to Question 1 give students some flexibility in writing their rules as they best see them.

Most likely, students will use one variable, for example B, for the population at the beginning of the time period and another, for example E, for the population at the end of the time period. They would then express the rule by an equation such as $E = 0.1B$ or $E = B - \frac{9}{10}B$.

Note: Estimates of the Native American population in 1492 vary widely, from 800,000 to 30,000,000. The 1900 census put the Native American population at 237,000.

If students have trouble finding a rule, ask, "How did you get the numerical results in Questions 2a and 2b?"

Question 2 is more difficult because it involves two input variables. If students have trouble finding a rule for their table, have them describe in words what they did to get their numerical results in Questions 2a and 2b. You should work with students on this, as needed, using the numerical examples of their work on Questions 2a and 2b to establish an arithmetic pattern.

They should be able to produce an equation like $N = 0.95A + 0.9C$ to describe what is happening, although some students may not yet be completely comfortable with this algebraic symbolism.

Someone may point out that it doesn't make sense for the output from this table to be anything other than a whole number. You can let the class come up with a way to resolve this dilemma, such as rounding off to the next highest integer.

Note: A supplemental problem, *Integers Only*, introduces the name and notation for the greatest integer function. Interested students might try to use this function to create a formula for Question 2c.

• Death on the trail

Have groups calculate how the results of this assignment affect their own Overland Trail families, based on whatever decision the class makes about rounding off results. You may want to have them treat their four families as a unit in determining how many people die, and then let them decide which families must suffer the deaths. They should put this information into their folders.

3. Wagon Train Sketches and Situations
(see next page)

The aim of this activity is to let students see how a graph can be used to illustrate a relationship between two different quantities, such as number of people and number of shoes needed, amount of time on the trail and amount of coffee consumed, and so forth.

The activity may work best as a mixture of group discussion and discussion involving the entire class.

In the activity, students will be interpreting graphs in a qualitative way, focusing on rise and fall. (In later activities, they will add scales, plot points, and draw graphs of equations on a set of coordinate axes.) *Wagon Train Sketches and*

Situations is aimed at motivating students to see the usefulness of drawing graphs. The activity uses the term *graph sketches* to describe these "unquantified" graphs.

As the activity states, the class wagon train has now arrived in Fort·Laramie, where they see a promotion poster with information about the journey westward in the form of graphs. Students will need to interpret the graph sketches, determining what each one means.

Then, reversing the procedure, they will create graph sketches to reflect information describing various relationships.

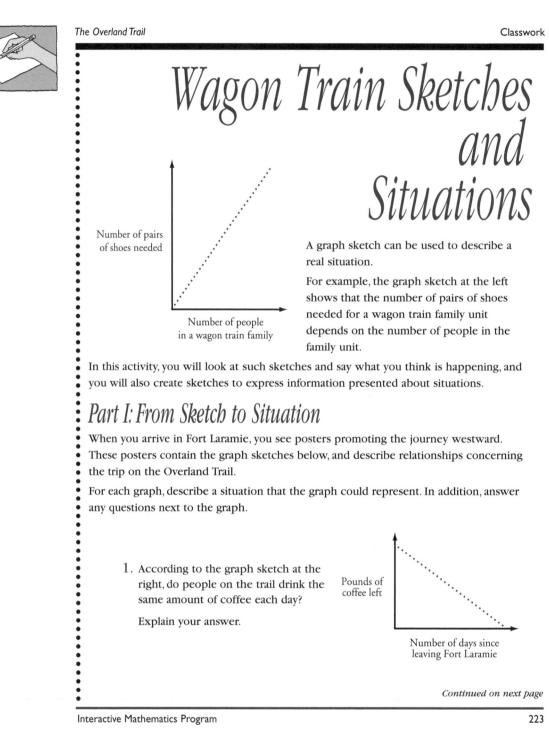

Wagon Train Sketches and Situations

A graph sketch can be used to describe a real situation.

For example, the graph sketch at the left shows that the number of pairs of shoes needed for a wagon train family unit depends on the number of people in the family unit.

In this activity, you will look at such sketches and say what you think is happening, and you will also create sketches to express information presented about situations.

Part I: From Sketch to Situation

When you arrive in Fort Laramie, you see posters promoting the journey westward. These posters contain the graph sketches below, and describe relationships concerning the trip on the Overland Trail.

For each graph, describe a situation that the graph could represent. In addition, answer any questions next to the graph.

1. According to the graph sketch at the right, do people on the trail drink the same amount of coffee each day?

   Explain your answer.

Continued on next page

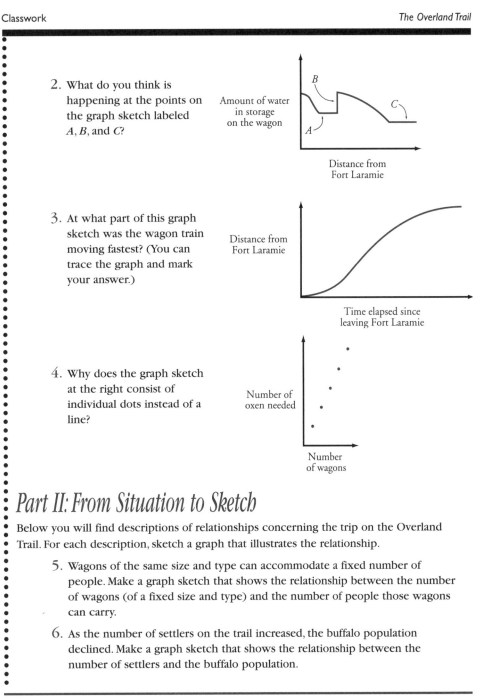

2. What do you think is happening at the points on the graph sketch labeled *A*, *B*, and *C*?

3. At what part of this graph sketch was the wagon train moving fastest? (You can trace the graph and mark your answer.)

4. Why does the graph sketch at the right consist of individual dots instead of a line?

Part II: From Situation to Sketch

Below you will find descriptions of relationships concerning the trip on the Overland Trail. For each description, sketch a graph that illustrates the relationship.

5. Wagons of the same size and type can accommodate a fixed number of people. Make a graph sketch that shows the relationship between the number of wagons (of a fixed size and type) and the number of people those wagons can carry.

6. As the number of settlers on the trail increased, the buffalo population declined. Make a graph sketch that shows the relationship between the number of settlers and the buffalo population.

224

It's probably best to start this activity as a whole class in order to get the students going. Ask students what the *shoes versus people* graph at the top of the activity tells them. (See "Assumptions on student preparation" below.)

There are at least a couple of observations that are fairly sure to come out.

- The more people there are, the more shoes are needed. (Brilliant!)

- The relationship is **linear**; that is, the dots are in a straight line.

Note: For now the term *linear* should be understood simply in its geometric sense. Students may not know the algebraic meaning of the term, and you should not introduce it. You may want to tell students that they will explore another meaning for "linear" later in this unit (and in other units). Specifically, they will see that certain algebraic rules correspond to straight line graphs.

You can continue the discussion of the *shoes versus people* graph as long as students are interested and have ideas to contribute. Then have students begin work in their groups on the other problems in *Wagon Train Sketches and Situations,* reminding them to keep a written record of their ideas.

As you circulate around the room, you can ask groups for explanations of the phenomena described in the graphs; that is, ask what might be happening to cause the graph to behave in a given way. The section below, titled "Discussion of *Wagon Train Sketches and Situations,*" contains suggestions that may be helpful in your interactions with the individual groups.

Make sure that students are not only answering the specific questions, but are also describing a situation for each graph.

- *Assumptions on student preparation*

This unit assumes that students are generally familiar with the coordinate system. They should know that the vertical and horizontal axes are thought of as resembling number lines and that each point in the coordinate plane corresponds to a pair of numbers, one on each axis. Although the axes in *Wagon Train Sketches and Situations* do not have numerical scales, students need to think of them as representing numerical information, the numbers increasing as one moves up or to the right.

Formal terminology about graphs will be introduced at appropriate times over the course of the unit.

Note: If you have students for which this complex of ideas is completely new, you may need to fill in some background information.

4. Discussion of Wagon Train Sketches and Situations

• Part I

As we stated earlier, you need not discuss each of the problems as a whole class, although it may be fruitful to have students give short presentations for some of the problems. The following commentary on Questions 1 through 4 provides ideas to look for if you have a whole-class discussion or as you circulate among groups.

Question 1. Students should be able to deduce from the linearity of this graph that coffee consumption is the same each day. They may express this by saying that the graph goes down the same amount for each day. (Students may not think that the graph is realistic, but they should realize that the graph does show the same amount of coffee being consumed each day.) You should informally use a phrase such as a "constant rate" in the context of this problem.

Note: Students will see a variety of situations involving constant rates before the formal concept of slope is introduced in the Year 3 unit *Small World, Isn't It?* The term *slope* is mentioned in passing on Day 16 of this unit.

Question 2. Students may have various theories about what is happening in this graph sketch.

One reasonable theory about the horizontal portions of this graph

sketch is that the wagon train group was traveling along a river and got their water from the river rather than from the water barrels.

So point *A* would represent arrival at the river, point *B* would represent people filling up their barrels before leaving the river, and point *C* would represent a time when they were traveling along another river.

Question 3. Students should be able to articulate that the wagon train is moving fastest when the graph is "steepest." You can ask them what might cause the changes in the speed of the wagon train's travel (terrain, weather, and so forth).

You can also ask what the graph sketch would look like if the wagon train had covered the same distance at a constant speed.

Question 4. This graph consists of individual points because the number of wagons must be a whole number.

Introduce the term **discrete** for a graph that consists of individual points.

You can bring out the contrast between the graph in Question 4 and the graph in Question 3, which was unbroken because the time and distance concepts make sense for any number including fractions. Introduce the term

continuous for a graph that is unbroken. You can reinforce the vocabulary by asking which of the other graphs in the activity are discrete and which are continuous.

> Students do not need to memorize definitions of these terms, but they should be aware of the distinction since it can help them understand what the graph is about.
>
> *Reminder:* Whenever you think vocabulary is important, you can post it somewhere in the room for reinforcement. You might want to include copies of graph sketches for Questions 3 and 4 with such a poster, since examples are often a better learning aid than formal definitions.

• *Part II*

Let one or two students present their sketches for each situation.

5. Independent and Dependent Variables

One issue that may come up in the discussion of *Wagon Train Sketches and Situations* is which axis to use for which variable. If it doesn't come up, raise it yourself.

Tell students that in many situations, one of the variables is *dependent* on the other. For example, the number of pairs of shoes needed depends on how many people there are in the family. (It may depend on other things as well, but that's an additional complication.)

Introduce the terms **independent variable** and **dependent variable**, and tell students that these are essentially synonymous with the *input* and *output* of an In-Out table.

Also tell them that the convention is to put the independent variable along the horizontal axis and to put the dependent variable along the vertical axis.

Homework 11: Graph Sketches
(see facing page)

Tonight's homework continues the work from *Wagon Train Sketches and Situations*. You may want to suggest that students put their work for Part II on index cards, to facilitate an exchange of problems in tomorrow's discussion.

Homework 11   Graph Sketches

Part I: Sketches to Situations

Each of the graph sketches below illustrates a relationship between two quantities. In each case, describe a situation that is illustrated by the graph.

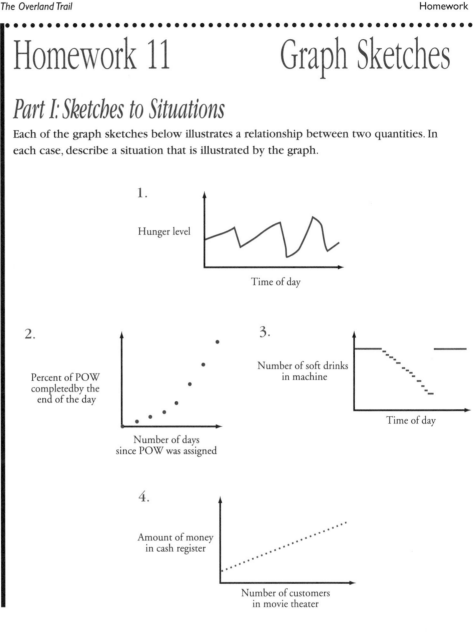

1.

Hunger level

Time of day

2.

Percent of POW completedby the end of the day

Number of days since POW was assigned

3.

Number of soft drinks in machine

Time of day

4.

Amount of money in cash register

Number of customers in movie theater

Continued on next page

Part II: Situations and Sketches

Begin with a situation in which you describe a possible relationship between two quantities.

Put this description on a separate piece of paper, and on the back, sketch the appropriate graph for that relationship. Remember to label the axes.

---

226   Interactive Mathematics Program

In Need of Numbers

Mathematical Topics

• Quantifying graphs using scales

Outline of the Day

In Class

1. Discuss *Homework 11: Graph Sketches*

2. Introduce *In Need of Numbers*
   • Use an example from *Wagon Train Sketches and Situations* to illustrate putting scales on axes

3. *In Need of Numbers*
   • Students add scales to their graph sketches
   • No whole-class discussion of this activity is needed

At Home

Homework 12: The Issues Involved

1. Discussion of Homework 11: Graph Sketches

You can allow time for students to discuss and share their opinions in their groups about Questions 1 through 4 of the homework. Your experience of yesterday's work on *Wagon Train Sketches and Situations* should determine the extent to which these problems are discussed as a whole class. One new mathematical idea that was introduced was the concept of a **step function** in Question 3.

The students may have imaginative descriptions to accompany the sketches they drew for homework. You can have each group pass their papers from Part II to the next group with the description face up. Each group should attempt to make a sketch that illustrates the description, and then compare their graph sketch with the one provided by the creator of the problem.

There will probably be disagreement on whose answer is "correct." As you circulate, emphasize that there can often be more than one correct graphical

2. Introduction to *In Need of Numbers*

interpretation of the description. See how well the activity goes and stop when you see fit. There is no need to do every graph sketch.

The purpose of the next activity, *In Need of Numbers,* is to get the students to add reasonable numerical scales to the axes of some of the graph sketches from yesterday's classwork and homework. You can use Question 1 from yesterday's *Wagon Train Sketches and Situations* (showing *pounds of coffee left versus the number of days since leaving Fort Laramie*) as an example for the whole class so that students will see the level of thought and detail you want. The initial, unscaled graph looked like this.

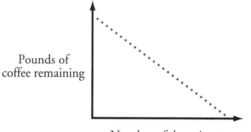

"What do you think would be an appropriate scale?"

Students will need to make estimates in order to choose an appropriate scale. For example, if they have the family start with 25 pounds of coffee and consume half a pound of coffee per day (perhaps for a large Overland Trail family), then the family will run out of coffee after 50 days. For those values, the graph with scaled axes might look like this.

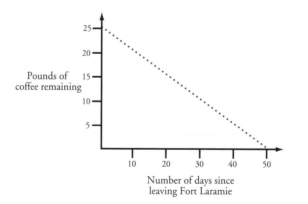

"Is it okay if '10 days' and '10 pounds' are represented by different lengths on the axes?"

You can pose the question whether it's permissible for "10 days" and "10 pounds" to be represented by different lengths on the two axes. You can tell students that if the units are not measuring the same type of item, then there is no reason for the lengths to match.

"How much coffee is left on the tenth day? The twentieth day?"

Once the class has decided how the axes will be scaled, you can ask specific questions, such as "How much coffee is left on the tenth day? The twentieth day?" and so on. Students can put the answers into an In-Out table, and then look for a rule for the In-Out table.

3. In Need of Numbers
(see next page)

After this introduction, students should proceed to work on the graph sketches in *In Need of Numbers,* and spend the rest of the class period on the activity.

> You do not need to discuss the activity with the whole class. Tonight's homework raises general issues about creating scales that may lead the class to look back at the graph sketches in *In Need of Numbers.*

Homework 12: The Issues Involved
(see page 90)

> The purpose of tonight's homework is to raise some general issues about the scaling of graphs.

In Need of Numbers

Graph sketches describe a situation, but the description would be more complete if the graph included numerical information.

You can do this by putting a **scale** on each axis, showing the numerical values that the points on each axis represent.

To scale an axis, you have to decide what range of values is appropriate for the particular situation and for the quantities involved. You also have to decide how to display the scale on each axis.

For each of the sketches illustrated on the next page, go through the three steps listed below.

• Make a copy of the sketch on graph paper.

• On your copy, scale the axes with appropriate values.

• Write down why your scales are reasonable and what assumptions you had to make.

Continued on next page

Interactive Mathematics Program   227

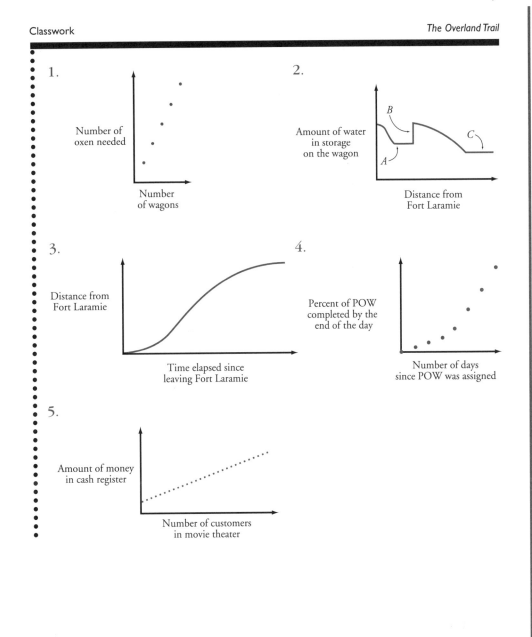

Homework 12   The Issues Involved

1. In *In Need of Numbers,* you put appropriate scales on the axes of different graphs.

   Make a list of difficulties you had and questions you would like answered that are related to scaling the axes of a graph.

The following questions will help you think in more detail about graphs and scaling. Use examples to explain your thinking and be detailed in your explanations.

2. Should the vertical axis always begin at zero? What is the effect if the axis does not begin at zero? What about the horizontal axis?

3. How do you decide what numbers to write along the axes?

4. The graph at the right shows the average height of boys in the United States at different ages.

   The graph appears to suggest that boys grow at a constant rate through age five.

   a. Why might someone make this conclusion from a quick glance at the graph?

   b. Why is this an incorrect conclusion?

   c. Redraw the graph so it is not misleading.

5. Suppose you wanted to sketch a graph showing the number of livestock deaths during the Overland Trail trip. Would you use a continuous or a discrete graph to represent this situation? Why?

Out Numbered

Students continue to work with numerical scales for graphs.

Mathematical Topics

- Issues related to scaling axes
- Reading information from a graph
- Using ordered pairs to represent points on a graph

Outline of the Day

In Class

1. Select presenters for tomorrow's discussion of *POW 9: Around the Horn*

2. Discuss *Homework 12: The Issues Involved*
   - Bring out that certain aspects of scaling are conventional, rather than "right" or "wrong," but that it is important that graphs not be misleading
   - Introduce the terms **first** and **second coordinates**, **coordinate axes**, and **ordered pair**

3. *Out Numbered*
   - Students read data from scaled graphs of linear situations and find rules for the data

4. Discuss *Out Numbered*
   - Emphasize that the straightness of the graph corresponds to a constant rate

At Home

Homework 13: Situations, Graphs, Rules, and Tables

1. POW Presentation Preparation

Presentations of *POW 9: Around the Horn* are scheduled for tomorrow. Choose three students to make POW presentations, and give them pens and overhead transparencies to take home to use in their preparations.

2. Discussion of *Homework 12: The Issues Involved*

Let students share their questions and problems from Question 1 within their groups and try to answer each other's questions. At the same time, assign each group one of Questions 2 through 5 to present to the class.

"What problems or questions did you have scaling the axes? Did you resolve them?"

After groups have had a chance to share ideas and get ready, go from group to group and ask each group to state one of the questions or difficulties they encountered relating to the scaling of axes.

If the group resolved the question, they should share the answer or solution they found.

Keep a list of unresolved questions. Some of them might be answered while discussing Questions 2 through 5, so you can wait until after those questions have been discussed before returning to this list.

• Question 2

In Question 2, tell students (if they don't realize it themselves) that there is no absolute rule for whether the vertical axis should begin at zero—it is really a judgment call. The same is true for the horizontal axis.

Point out that in some cases starting a scale other than at zero gives a wrong impression of the data, while in other cases it does not.

Note: You may want to talk about the ethical issues of using misleading scales. However, this will be discussed more fully in the next unit, *The Pit and the Pendulum*—see *Homework 17: A Picture Is Worth a Thousand Words*.

• Question 3

In Question 3, there is once again no clear answer. There needs to be enough information shown to give a sense of scale, but beyond that, it is a judgment call as to what would make a graph more readable and what would clutter it up. Students should be made aware that they do not have to write out every integer!

• Question 4

At this point, students should be able to connect the faulty conclusion that boys grow at a constant rate through age five with the apparent straight line graph. They will presumably see that the conclusion is faulty because the uneven labeling along the vertical axis creates a distortion of the graph.

"How much does an average boy grow in his first year? In his second year?"

You may want to ask explicitly how much an average boy grows in his first year, second year, and so on, both to focus on graph reading skills and to clarify that the amount decreases from year to year.

You can tell students that the scales in this graph are considered deceptive. Unless there is a very compelling reason to do otherwise, we always mark scales so that equal distances on a given scale correspond to equal amounts (just as we do on a simple number line).

Note: This is a different issue from whether the scale on the vertical axis should be the same as the scale on the horizontal axis.

The group presenting Question 4 should provide a new graph with appropriate scales. Such a graph might look like this.

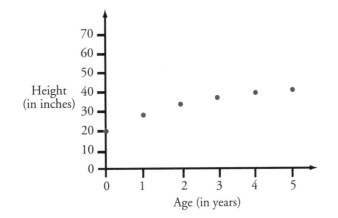

• *Question 5*

In Question 5, students need to realize that the issue of whether a graph is *discrete* or *continuous* usually depends on the context of the problem. You can use this occasion to review that the terms *discrete* and *continuous*.

If the independent variable represents something that is counted with whole numbers, then the graph will consist of individual points.

Note: If the independent variable is continuous but the dependent variable is discrete, the result might be a step function as in Question 3 of *Homework 11: Graph Sketches.*

Caution students that at times, graphs that should be discrete are presented as continuous, for any of several reasons: because the scale used makes it impossible to draw so many dots; because the graph is more readable without dots; or just because it simplifies the problem.

• *General terms and ideas*

As needed, tell students that the two numbers associated with a point on a graph are called its **coordinates**, with the number from the horizontal axis called the **first coordinate** and the number from the vertical axis called the **second coordinate.** The vertical and horizontal axes are sometimes referred to generically as **coordinate axes.**

Also tell students that we often represent a point on a graph by giving its two coordinates, and illustrate with an example. Suppose, for instance, in the *pounds of coffee versus days since leaving Fort Laramie* graph, that there are 15 pounds of coffee after 20 days. There is a point on the graph that corresponds to this information, and we represent that point as (20, 15).

"Why do you suppose an 'ordered pair' is called that?"

Tell students that this notation is called an **ordered pair**, and ask them to explain why the word *ordered* is used in this expression. (Answer: Because (20, 15) and (15, 20) represent different information.)

> *Comment:* All of this terminology and notation may already be familiar to most students, but it is probably worth taking a minute to review it.

"How is looking at a graph like looking at an In-Out table?"

Bring out that looking at a graph is like looking at an In-Out table—each point on the graph represents a pair of numbers, as does each row of an In-Out table. (Although students have seen tables with more than one input, you can ignore this complication here.)

You may want to remind students that we generally associate the horizontal axis with the *In* and the vertical axis with the *Out*. (See the section "Independent and Dependent Variables; Horizontal and Vertical Axes" on Day 11.)

3. *Out Numbered*
(see facing page)

> The activity *Out Numbered* focuses on the process of reading data from a graph and the connection between graphs and In-Out tables. This emphasis is continued in *Homework 14: Rules, Tables, and Graphs.*
>
> *Out Numbered* gives students an opportunity to solidify their understanding of the relationship between graphs and In-Out tables, and allows them to review their work in *Patterns* with writing rules for In-Out tables.

Let groups prepare presentations for parts d and e of each problem once they are ready. You may want to omit Question 1 to save time, since Questions 2 and 3 are more likely to need discussion.

Out Numbered

The scaled graphs in this activity are similar to examples you have seen before. Base your answers to the questions *on the scales shown in these graphs*.

1. This graph shows the number of people that can be carried in a given number of wagons.

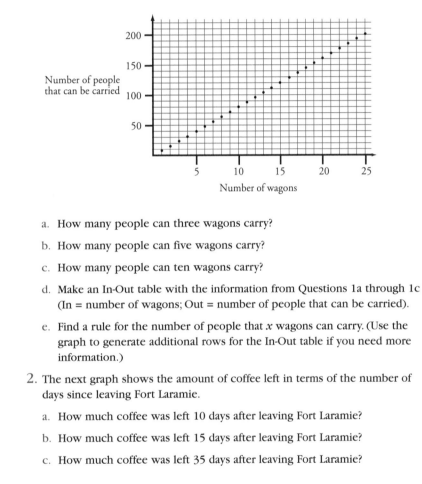

   a. How many people can three wagons carry?

   b. How many people can five wagons carry?

   c. How many people can ten wagons carry?

   d. Make an In-Out table with the information from Questions 1a through 1c (In = number of wagons; Out = number of people that can be carried).

   e. Find a rule for the number of people that *x* wagons can carry. (Use the graph to generate additional rows for the In-Out table if you need more information.)

2. The next graph shows the amount of coffee left in terms of the number of days since leaving Fort Laramie.

   a. How much coffee was left 10 days after leaving Fort Laramie?

   b. How much coffee was left 15 days after leaving Fort Laramie?

   c. How much coffee was left 35 days after leaving Fort Laramie?

Continued on next page

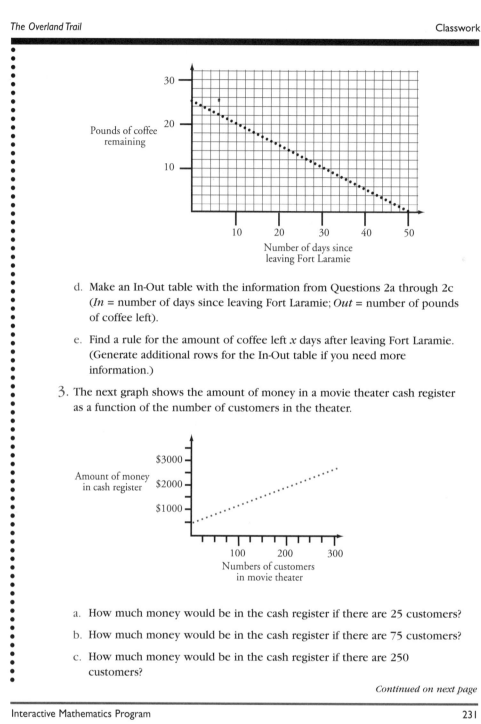

d. Make an In-Out table with the information from Questions 2a through 2c (*In* = number of days since leaving Fort Laramie; *Out* = number of pounds of coffee left).

e. Find a rule for the amount of coffee left *x* days after leaving Fort Laramie. (Generate additional rows for the In-Out table if you need more information.)

3. The next graph shows the amount of money in a movie theater cash register as a function of the number of customers in the theater.

a. How much money would be in the cash register if there are 25 customers?

b. How much money would be in the cash register if there are 75 customers?

c. How much money would be in the cash register if there are 250 customers?

Continued on next page

d. Make an In-Out table with the information from Questions 3a through 3c (*In* = number of customers; *Out* = amount of money in cash register).

e. Find a rule for the amount of money in the cash register if there are *x* customers. (Add more rows to the In-Out table if you need more information.)

4. Discussion of *Out Numbered*

"Why does the rule Out = 8 · In make sense in Question 1?" "How much coffee is consumed each day in Question 2?" "What is the cost of admission in Question 3?"

Use the presentations as an opportunity to connect the rules directly to the situations. For example,

- In Question 1, try to get students to see that a rule such as *Out = 8 · In* makes sense because each wagon holds the same number of people.

- In Question 2, ask students how much coffee is being consumed each day.

- In Question 3, ask what the cost of admission is.

In all three problems, the linearity of the graph reflects the fact that the situation involves a constant rate. (This connection was addressed on Day 11 in the discussion of *Wagon Train Sketches and Situations*.) As students discuss *Out Numbered*, focus on how the rules provide a way to describe the situations rather than on any formal procedure for getting such rules from In-Out tables.

Homewok 13   Situations, Graphs, Tables, and Rules

In *Out Numbered,* you used three different ways to represent a situation.

- A graph
- An In-Out table
- A rule for the table

The relationships between these three forms of representation, and the relationship of each to the original situation, are among the most fundamental ideas in mathematics.

In *Patterns* you expressed real-world situations by using In-Out tables and found rules for the tables. In this unit you have been using *graphs* to represent situations.

Explain how the four ideas—situations, graphs, In-Out tables, and rules—relate to one another. Use examples from this unit and examples of your own to show how you can go from one form of representation to another.

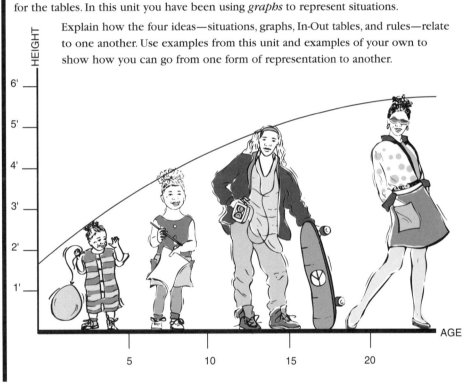

Homework 13:
Situations, Graphs, Tables, and Rules

Tonight's homework gives students a chance to synthesize and reflect on the connections between three different ways of representing a situation. The assignment will be included in students' portfolios for the unit.

DAY 14

POW 9 Presentations

Students present POW 9.

Mathematical Topics

* Understanding the connections between situations, graphs, In-Out tables, and algebraic rules

Outline of the Day

In Class

1. Discuss *Homework 13: Situations, Graphs, Tables, and Rules*
   * Optional: Have each group start with an example of one of the four categories and then create the others to match
2. Presentations of *POW 9: Around the Horn*

* Discuss students' different interpretations of how to count ships at the beginning and at the end of a trip

At Home

Homework 14: Rules, Tables, and Graphs

POW 10: On Your Own (due Day 24)

1. Discussion of *Homework 13: Situations, Graphs, Tables, and Rules*

You can ask for volunteers to read their homework papers to the class.

There are many different ways that students might respond to the assignment, and you should use their responses as feedback to determine how well they understand the connections between situations, graphs, In-Out tables, and algebraic rules.

Although you should take care to clear up any misunderstandings, you should not expect students to provide definitive statements about the relationships between these ideas.

Here are examples of the type of general descriptive statement to look for.

- In-Out tables give specific points for a graph.

- A rule describes the relationship between the *Out* and the *In*.

- A graph is a pictorial representation of a situation.

If students don't come up with statements like these, then perhaps they are not yet ready to formulate their ideas in a theoretical way and need more experience working with examples of the different forms of representation. You should keep in mind that these ideas are used in all four years of the IMP curriculum, and students will see them many times again.

- *A suggestion for discussing "Homework 13: Situations, Graphs, Tables, and Rules"*

You may find it productive to assign one of the four categories—situation, graph, table, or rule—to each group and to ask them to create something for their category and then to create the other three items to go with it.

For example, if a group is assigned the category "table," they would begin by making an In-Out table, then make a graph for their table, find a rule for the table, and make up a situation to go with the table.

Although some parts of this process may be difficult, the approach may help to establish the connections between the concepts more clearly than the abstract discussion called for in last night's homework.

2. Presentations of POW 9: Around the Horn

Have the three students selected yesterday present their ideas about the POW. It will probably be helpful if they act out the movement of ships from one coast to another.

"What assumptions did you make?"

There may be disagreement about whether to count the ships that are arriving as a student leaves and those that are leaving as the student arrives. The problem is ambiguous in this respect, so there is more than one correct answer. Students should state their assumptions in their presentations.

"How could you generalize your results?"

After the presentations, you can ask the students how they could generalize their results. For instance, ask what formulas they can come up with that will describe how to find answers to problems of this type.

Homework 14

Rules, Tables, and Graphs

In *Out Numbered,* you started from graphs, made In-Out tables, and then found rules for those tables.

This process can be reversed. You can start from a rule, make an In-Out table by finding pairs of numbers that fit the rule, and then create a graph from the table.

By convention, we find the *In* on the horizontal axis and the *Out* on the vertical axis. So each pair of numbers that fits the rule corresponds to a point on the graph.

Continued on next page

Homework 14: *Rules, Tables, and Graphs*

In *Out Numbered,* students started from graphs, made In-Out tables, and then found rules for those tables. This assignment reverses the process, and gives students a sense of what is meant by "the graph of an equation."

The *In* and *Out* values are called the **first** and **second coordinates** of the point on the graph. The graph consists of all the points that correspond to number pairs that fit the rule.

In these problems, do not restrict yourself to whole numbers. Consider all numbers, including negative and noninteger values.

1. You came across many different In-Out rules in *Patterns*. Sometimes the rules came from problem situations. Sometimes you looked at rules that had no particular context.

   For each of the rules below, find as many points on the graph as you think you need to get an idea of what the whole graph looks like. Then draw the graph.

   a. *Out* = 4 · *In* – 4 (this rule occurred in *Homework 21: The Garden Border* in *Patterns*)

   b. *Out* = *In*^{2} (this rule relates to area, among other things)

   c. *Out* = 550 – 20 · *In*

2. The concept of a graph can also be applied to an equation that does not directly express an *Out* in terms of an *In*.

   For each of the equations shown below,

   • find some number pairs that fit the equation

   • make a graph from your number pairs, using the *x*-value as the first coordinate and the *y*-value as the second coordinate

   a. $3x + 2y = 9$

   b. $y^2 = x$

Question 2 is the first time in the IMP curriculum that students have seen such "naked" equations involving variables. Students generally make this transition easily, but you might take a minute to have students give one or two examples of number pairs that fit each equation.

POW 10:
On Your Own
(see next page)

This POW has a very different flavor from others that students have done, because it does not involve solving a mathematics problem.

One purpose of the assignment is to get students to put mathematics to practical use. Another is to help them develop organizational skills.

You may want to suggest that students work in pairs on this POW, perhaps pretending they are going to be roommates sharing an apartment. They may prefer to choose partners who are not in their usual groups.

Make it clear that each student needs to prepare an individual report, even if two students work together on the POW.

Students will have about two weeks to work on the POW. We suggest that you get a progress report from students on Day 19.

Students will discuss *POW 10: On Your Own* in their usual groups on Day 24.

POW 10 *On Your Own*

One of the key themes of this unit is that of planning. You have planned a lunch and you have planned what supplies your wagon train needs to bring.

One reason for doing such assignments is so that you can get better at organizing details. Another is so you can get better at asking yourself questions like "What will I need?" and at developing responses to such questions.

This is a research POW. You are to go out and find information. Your topic? Living on your own.

Imagine that you have just completed high school. There may have been adults who took care of many things for you before, but now you want to move out on your own.

Continued on next page

For the purpose of this assignment, assume that you need to provide your own financial support. What sorts of things do you need to plan for?

Be very detailed and accurate in your plan. If you are going to get your own apartment, then find an example of one in the classified section of a newspaper and find the cost. You will need a job—a job that you can enter with a high school education. You will need to know what you would get paid and how much of that is "take-home pay."

It will probably be helpful to you to interview people for this POW. There is nothing like experience. What bills are you going to have to pay? Does your apartment rent include the cost of electricity? People already living on their own will be able to share with you how they manage the bills.

Your report should include a budget, which is a plan for how your money is going to be spent on a month-to-month basis.

Good luck!

Write-up

Since this is not a standard POW, you can't use the standard POW write-up. Use the categories listed below instead.

1. *Description of the Task:* Explain in your own words what you are trying to do in this POW.

2. *Your Job:* You can consider such questions as

   - What is the job?

   - How do you find it?

   - What are your hours and salary?

3. *Your Living Arrangement:* Would you live with roommates? By yourself? What about furniture?

4. *A Monthly Budget:* Include more than just numbers. Discuss how and why you decided on your budget and where you got your information.

5. *Evaluation:* Did you enjoy doing this POW? In what ways do you think it will be helpful to you in the future?

Days 15-18

Making Predictions with Graphs

This page in the student book introduces Days 15 through 18.

Graphs don't just tell stories; they can also be very useful in making predictions. The lives of travelers on the Overland Trail often depended on their ability to accurately foresee what could happen to them. The data they worked with didn't fit formulas as neatly as data in textbook problems, so they had to make approximations.

As travelers set out from Fort Laramie toward Fort Hall, Idaho, one of the decisions they made involved a shortcut called Sublette's Cutoff. When you get there, think about what choice you might have made.

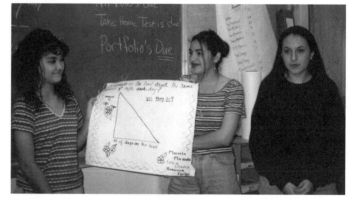

Mariela Miranda, Erica Chavez, and Roxanne Farler present their graph to the class.

Previous Travelers

Students look intuitively for lines of best fit for some Overland Trail data.

Mathematical Topics

- Graphing algebraic functions and equations
- Formal introduction of the coordinate system, including terminology of quadrants
- Distinguishing graphs of functions from arbitrary sets of points
- Using tables of information and lines of best fit to make predictions and estimates
- Making a graph from tabular information

Outline of the Day

In Class

1. Discuss *Homework 14: Rules, Tables, and Graphs*
   - Introduce the terms **parabola**, **rectangular** (or **Cartesian**) **coordinate system**, **quadrant**
   - Review the distinction between a function and an arbitrary graph or set of pairs
2. *Previous Travelers*
   - Students plot data, look for lines of best fit and rules for those lines, and make predictions based on those rules

- Introduce the activity
  - ✔ Set the geographic context
  - ✔ Have students plot points for *people versus beans* and save their graphs for possible use tomorrow
  - ✔ Give an intuitive introduction to the idea of **line of best fit**
- Part I of the activity will be completed and discussed on Day 16
- Part II will be done on Day 16

At Home

Homework 15: Broken Promises

Special Materials Needed

- Clear straightedges or raw spaghetti (useful for finding lines of best fit)

Discuss With Your Colleagues

Why Not Regression Now?

When students begin to find lines of best fit, it may be tempting to introduce the class to the regression feature of the graphing calculator. The IMP curriculum delays the use of this calculator shortcut until Year 3.

Discuss the advantages and disadvantages of this curriculum decision.

1. Discussion of *Homework 14: Rules, Tables, and Graphs*

Give students some time to compare their graphs and then have diamond card students from different groups present their results.

For the most part, these problems are fairly straightforward, but they offer an opportunity to review or introduce some fundamental concepts and terms used in graphing. Many of the ideas will be familiar to students, and a review of terms can either be interwoven with the individual examples or discussed when the presentations are completed.

There are no special points that need to be made about the individual problems. Here, though, are a few specific points that you or the students could bring up:

• Only Questions 1a, 1c, and 2a have graphs that are straight lines. (Students may gradually be making a connection between the algebra and the geometry, but you need not push that now. The connection will emerge more explicitly in the next unit, *The Pit and the Pendulum.*)

• You can introduce the word **parabola** for the shape of the graph in Question 1b.

• The graph in Question 2b has the same shape as that in Question 1b, but opens in a different direction.

Note: In the next unit, *The Pit and the Pendulum,* students will have a "graphing free-for-all" to explore what the graphs look like for a variety of functions.

• *The rectangular coordinate system*

Students should be finding points with both positive and negative coordinates. Introduce the synonymous terms **rectangular coordinate system** and **Cartesian coordinate system** for the standard graph set-up with a vertical and a horizontal axis.

Also, tell students that in the absence of any other information, the standard notation is to use *x* for the independent variable represented on the horizontal axis and to use *y* for the dependent variable represented on the vertical axis. (The terms *independent variable* and *dependent variable* were introduced on Day 11.)

Tell students also that unless there is a reason to do otherwise, we generally use the same scale on both axes.

• *Ordered pairs*

You can use this discussion as an opportunity to review the ordered pair notation introduced on Day 13. For example, in Question 1a, if a student says, "When the *In* is 3, the *Out* is 8," you can say, "So the point (3, 8) is on the graph."

• *The quadrants*

Introduce the term **quadrant** and the standard numbering system for the quadrants as shown below.

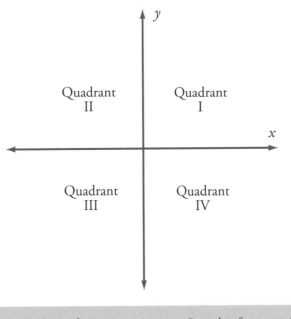

Students will be graphing functions throughout the IMP curriculum, and you need not worry about whether they memorize the numbering system now. Casual references in context—for example, "Which quadrants does this graph use?"—will gradually make students familiar with the system.

• *Function versus nonfunction*

One important point to make, particularly in connection with Question 2b, is that functions form a special category within the more general category of relationships.

Students were told in *Patterns* that not every In-Out table is considered a function. The explanation they were given is that a function cannot have more than one *Out* for a given *In*.

*"How is the graph
in Question 2b
different from all
the others?"*

You can focus on the distinction between function and nonfunction by asking how the graph in Question 2b is different from the others. If this question does not elicit the type of response you want, point out that there are different points on the graph that have the same *x*-coordinates, such as (4, 2) and (4, –2).

In other words, the graph in Question 2b is not the graph of a function. You can point out that whenever we have the *Out* explicitly in terms of the *In*, then we definitely have a function. In other cases, it isn't obvious. The equation in Question 2a does give a function, but the equation in Question 2b does not.

Note: In a sequence of problems beginning with *Fair Share on Chores* on Day 22, students will get experience transforming equations like the one in Question 2a into a form that explicitly gives one variable in terms of the other.

You might also refer back to Question 2 of *Wagon Train Sketches and Situations* (Day 11), in which the graph seems to show the amount of water in storage increasing while the wagon stays in the same place. In other words, the amount of water is not a *function* of the distance from Fort Laramie.

2. *Previous Travelers*
(see page 115)

The next several days' work (through *Homework 18: Out of Action*) forms something like a subunit, focusing on interpreting graphs and using them to make predictions and to solve problems. Students will go through the following stages, in which they

- transform information from tabular form or verbal description to graphical form

- look for a straight line that reasonably approximates the graph

- use a table for that straight line as an aid in finding a rule for the graph

- use the graph or the rule to make predictions and estimates about the situation described

Students will do a series of related problems, some set in the context of the Overland Trail and some set in other contexts.

In the activity *Previous Travelers,* students receive a letter giving them data about the consumption of various items by different families who have completed the trip. Today they will begin Part I, in which they analyze the information in the letter. On Day 16, they will complete and discuss Part I, and then work on Part II, making adjustments to their supplies for the next leg of the journey. The adjustments they decide to make will be based on their work in Part I.

Each group will need to record its decisions in Part II.

There are important new ideas introduced in the activity, and it is probably best to work through one example as a class. The commentary that follows provides suggestions on how to do this, and uses the commodity of beans as an example.

Before starting the activity, the class can take a minute to look at the map in order to place this section of the trip in geographical context. Fort Hall is in present-day Pocatello, Idaho.

• *Creating a graph*

"How would you make a graph for beans?"

Ask students to read through the activity. Then ask them how to make a graph for a selected item (for example, beans). As you work through this activity with them, it will be helpful if you create an overhead transparency of the graph, for use in today's discussion and for possible use tomorrow as well.

Students need to see that the table in the letter can be viewed as a shorthand for three separate tables, one for each item. If needed, create a separate In-Out table like the one below from the data in the activity.

Number of people	Number of pounds of beans
5	61
8	95
6	56
etc.	

There might be disagreement regarding which axis to use for which quantity. If so, remind students (as noted yesterday) that we generally associate the *In* with the horizontal axis and the *Out* with the vertical axis.

"How would you scale the axes?"

The class needs to decide how to scale the axes. Since they are asked to make predictions for the number of people in their own Overland Trail families, they should make sure that the horizontal scale goes up to the largest family size they will need.

They also need to realize that the vertical axis should include not only the numbers in the table itself, but the number of beans for the largest family size they will need.

Urge them to start both axes at zero. As discussed in *Homework 12: The Issues Involved*, starting an axis at a point other than zero can lead to distortion of the information.

• *Line of best fit*

"Where is the line that comes closest to the data?"

Once the points have been plotted, the class then needs to pick a **line of best fit.** Use this phrase and explain it intuitively through a demonstration. You can place a pencil (or other narrow straightedge, such as a piece of raw spaghetti) on the overhead projector, move it around, and have the class tell you when to stop so that the pencil is in the best position to represent the data.

Keep the decision about the placement of the line intuitive, and acknowledge that the question of "best" placement is a subjective one. Later in this unit, students will find lines of best fit by plotting data with a graphing calculator and by using a trial-and-error approach to find a function whose graph closely fits the data. In that work, the judgment as to what is "best" will still be subjective.

Note: You may want to mention that there are formal procedures for measuring how well a line or other type of function fits a set of data. Students will learn about this in Years 3 and 4 of the IMP curriculum. They will use a regression feature on the calculator to find functions of best fit and will learn about the method of least squares.

"Based on the line of best fit, how many pounds of beans will each of your Overland Trail families need?"

Draw the line of best fit and extend it far enough so that the amount of beans for each group's number of people can be found. Ask groups to read from the graph the number of pounds of beans that their Overland Trail families will need.

Save the graph for possible use in tomorrow's discussion.

• *A rule for the line*

"Can you write an algebraic rule for your line of best fit?"

Next, turn students' attention to finding a rule for the line of best fit. Create a new In-Out table by looking at some points spread out along the line and reading their coordinates. The rule will be something like this:

number of pounds of beans = 12 • (number of people)

This equation can be used to find the amount of beans needed for larger groups that do not fit on the graph. For example, a group can find the total needed for their four combined families or for the class wagon train as a whole.

• *Groups work on remaining items*

There will probably not be enough time for all three supply items to be graphed and analyzed by the groups in class. Students will have more time to work on this in class tomorrow, and will discuss it then as well.

Previous Travelers

The first settlers had to make the long journey west without any help from previous travelers. However, subsequent wagon trains used information from the early travelers to decide on the quantity of supplies appropriate for their journey.

The Letter

While in Fort Laramie, Wyoming, you get the letter below from friends describing the supplies they and others used on the leg of the trip from Fort Laramie to Fort Hall, Idaho.

Continued on next page

Interactive Mathematics Program

239

Dear friends:

We've arrived in Fort Hall after many adventures, both good and bad. It would take me forever to describe all that happened, so we can talk about all of that when we meet up again in California.

I know that you're anxious for some practical information for your own trip. Several of the families on our wagon train kept track of the quantities of various goods they actually needed on the journey. The families were of different sizes, so this information should help you and your friends decide how the amounts vary from group to group. I know this won't answer all your questions, but it's a start.

Number of people	Pounds of gunpowder	Pounds of sugar	Pounds of beans
5	3	20	61
8	4	50	95
6	2.5	30	56
7	4.1	23	75
11	5	60	125
10	5.8	40	135
5	1.8	39	80
7	3.8	44	100
10	4.3	53	103
6	3.6	35	75
8	3.2	35	100
7	3.1	36	105
9	4.7	45	125
12	6.1	55	150
10	5.2	31	125

Well, good luck to you all!

The Helmicks

Continued on next page

Part I: The Analysis

1. Make a separate graph for each of the supply items needed, using appropriate scales for the axes.

2. Do the following tasks for each of the graphs in Question 1.

   a. Sketch the **line of best fit** for the graph; that is, find the straight line that you think best fits the data.

   b. Make an In-Out table *from your line* and determine the rule for the In-Out table.

   c. Use either the In-Out table or your graph to find the quantity of each item needed for each of your group's four family units.

Part II: More Planning

3. In *Planning for the Long Journey,* you decided on supply amounts of gunpowder, sugar, and beans for the trip from Westport to Fort Laramie. Through good fortune or the generosity of others, you made it successfully so far, but you have used up those initial supplies.

   The same supplies, in the same quantities, were ordered in advance to be ready for you here at Fort Laramie, and you picked up those supplies on your arrival yesterday. Now that you have analyzed the information from the Helmicks, you need to rethink your provisions.

   Compare the supply amounts found in Question 2c for gunpowder, sugar, and beans to the amounts you decided on in *Planning for the Long Journey* and which you now have again for the next leg of the trip, from Fort Laramie to Fort Hall.

   If your supply of a certain item is not what it should be, then you will need to trade for more of that item with another group. (The trading post has run out of supplies, so you can't buy more there.)

   Warning: If you fail to get sufficient supplies, then some members of your Overland Trail family might perish before you get to Fort Hall.

Homework 15   Broken Promises

1492

Over the years, Native Americans were forced onto smaller and smaller parcels of land. Though the United States government signed treaties with the native peoples, the government repeatedly broke those treaties.

The maps at the left and below show the outline of the contiguous 48 states of the United States. The colored portion represents the extent of Native American land within this area at different times.

1790

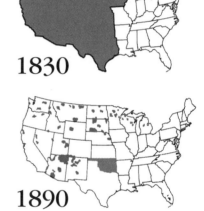

1830

1860

1890

Maps reproduced by permission of Thunderbird Enterprises, Phoenix, Arizona.

Continued on next page

Homework 15: Broken Promises

Students may need to be reminded of how area is measured. You may want to point out the suggestion made in Question 1 of the homework that students copy each diagram onto a sheet of graph paper and use one square as a unit of area.

1. Approximate the area of Native American land at each of the given times. The total area shown for 1492 is approximately 3,000,000 square miles. (*Suggestion:* You may want to trace each map onto grid paper and use one square as the unit of area.)

2. Make a graph showing the relationship between the passage of time and the area of Native American land. (Be careful to use appropriate spacing on your time interval.)

3. If it were 1861 and you were only looking at the maps of what had happened so far, what would you predict as the area of Native American land in the year 2020?

4. What prediction might you have made in 1900 about Native American land in the year 2020?

Previous Travelers Continued

Students continue finding lines of best fit for Overland Trail supply data, and use the lines to make estimates.

Mathematical Topics

- Extracting information from graphs
- Using information from graphs to make predictions
- Dealing with ambiguous situations
- Acting out mathematics problems

Outline of the Day

In Class

1. Discuss *Homework 15: Broken Promises*
   - Compare methods for estimating areas

2. Complete and discuss Part I of *Previous Travelers* (from Day 15)
   - Ask students to share their graphs and analyses for each supply item
   - Focus on the intuitive meaning of the line of best fit and on connections between graphs, rules, and tables
   - Groups need to determine the amount of each item needed for their families

3. *Previous Travelers,* Part II
   - Allow students to adjust their supplies from those preordered in *Planning the Long Journey,* basing their adjustments on their conclusions from *Previous Travelers*
   - Groups should record their new supply totals

At Home

Homework 16: Sublette's Cutoff

What About Slope?

Why not teach students how to get the equation of a straight line? Isn't that part of the ninth grade curriculum?

As with the use of variables, working with graphs involves laying a foundation of fundamental concepts, including the relationship between a situation, an In-Out table, an algebraic formulation, and a graph.

Discuss the difference in flavor between talking about "the amount of coffee used per day" and defining slope by the expression $\frac{y_2 - y_1}{x_2 - x_1}$.

1. Discussion of *Homework 15: Broken Promises*

Let students compare results in their groups, and then bring them together as a whole class.

"How did you estimate the areas?"

You may want to take a few minutes to talk about their techniques for estimating the areas, and about the way they set up the scales on the axes.

Then turn to Questions 3 and 4. In Question 3, results will probably vary, depending on how carefully students estimated the areas and how they chose their lines of best fit.

"What was your prediction for 2020?"

Students probably decided in Question 4 that Native Americans would not have any land left in 2020. A linear approximation of the data suggests, in fact, that Native Americans would have no more land as early as the beginning of the twentieth century. This was not the case, however, and there was comparatively little net change in the amount of land possessed by Native Americans during the twentieth century. (This last statement is not meant to minimize the inequity of the situation.)

One conclusion to draw from this assignment is that looking at a graph out of context can be fairly meaningless in predicting real-world events.

2. Completion and Discussion of Part I of *Previous Travelers*

Groups should complete the work begun yesterday. As they finish, you can hand out overhead transparencies of graph paper and assign each group one of the supply items to present to the class.

• *Discussion*

The focus of the class discussion should be on the idea of the line of best fit and on the connections between graphs, tables, and rules.

"As you move along the line of best fit, how does the amount of beans increase as the number of people increases?"

Students should now have a clearer understanding of the direct connection between the graph and the rule. You can use the bean graph from yesterday and have the class imagine moving to the right along the line of best fit. Ask them how the amount of beans is increasing as the number of people increases. It should be apparent that for each additional person, about 12 more pounds of beans are required. (Student estimates may vary.) This is the key to a linear relationship—a constant rate of increase.

Groups may wish to recalculate how much gunpowder, sugar, and beans they need to bring for each of their Overland Trail families after they hear the presentations.

• *Steepness*

Tell the class that the "steepness" of a linear graph can be measured numerically by something called the **slope**, although the steepness depends on the scales of the axes as well as on the data involved. You can tell them that they will learn more about slope when they study rates of change in the Year 3 unit *Small World, Isn't It?*

Note: At this point, we do not want to get into a technical discussion of the concept of slope, but just want to begin to develop the students' intuitive understanding. Slope is an abstract algebraic concept, related to but distinct from the concept of rate in a problem setting. Discussion of slope at this point may mystify some students. We don't want the relationships among situation, graph, table, and rule to be complicated by technical details such as writing rules in the form $y = mx + b$.

3. *Previous Travelers, Part II*

In Part II of *Previous Travelers,* students need to look back at the supplies they purchased in the activity *Planning for the Long Journey* (on Days 5 and 6). As they were told then, and as *Previous Travelers* points out, they are being resupplied at Fort Laramie with those same supply amounts.

If these amounts are different from what their work on Part I suggests that they will need, they can trade supplies with other groups. You might let groups with cash left over from *Planning for the Long Journey* use the money to purchase more supplies (they should refer to the *Overland Trail Price List*).

Let students know that if they don't get sufficient supplies, members of their Overland Trail families might die before getting to Fort Hall. (The consequences of not having sufficient supplies are dealt with in the Day 20 discussion of *Homework 19: What We Needed.*)

For your information: The set of data in *Previous Travelers* suggests consumption of approximately 0.5 pounds of gunpowder, 5 pounds of sugar, and 12 pounds of beans per person for the journey from Fort Laramie to Fort Hall. If students get values substantially less than this, they will end up short of supplies when they do *Homework 19: What We Needed.*

If everyone is short on supplies, you may want to come up with an idea for making supplies available. For example, you can suggest that there was a last-minute delivery at Fort Laramie, and the government is providing a per-person allotment of gunpowder, sugar, and beans.

Students should record their current supplies in their folder (after trading, receiving additional provisions, and so forth). The information will be used on Day 20, in the discussion of *Homework 19: What We Needed.*

• *The data set in "Previous Travelers" does not form a function*

You can follow up this discussion by bringing out that the In-Out tables for the different items in *Previous Travelers* do not constitute functions.

For example, there are two families with five members apiece, and each family uses different amounts of gunpowder, sugar, and beans. So we cannot say that the amount used for one of these items is "a function of" the family size.

Instead, what students are doing in *Previous Travelers* is finding rules that give a reasonable approximation of the relationship between amount used and family size.

Keep in mind, however, that when students find a line of best fit, *that line* does represent a function.

Homework 16: Sublette's Cutoff
(see facing page)

Sublette's Cutoff started just west of South Pass, which was considered the halfway point on the trip to California. Once again, point out on a map where the wagons are on the journey. South Pass is near present-day Highway 28, south of Lander, Wyoming, along the Continental Divide.

Homework 16

Sublette's Cutoff

The Shortcut

As more and more emigrants made the journey west, scouts found shortcuts to lessen the travel time. Help provided by Native Americans in the area was also important in facilitating the journey.

The Shoshone, Assiniboin, and Crow nations were prominent in the area of what is now Wyoming and Idaho.

One such shortcut, along the way between Fort Laramie and Fort Hall, was known as Sublette's Cutoff. The cutoff began just past South Pass in Wyoming, about 250 miles west of Fort Laramie, and ended near the Wyoming-Idaho border.

Continued on next page

This shortcut saved 50 miles and a week of travel, but crossed a dry and barren stretch of land. It was a grueling route of 15 days with little grass and no water.

Your Problem

Three families decide to attempt to cross Sublette's Cutoff. The table below shows how much water each of these families has left at the end of the first, second, fourth, and sixth days.

Gallons of Water Remaining

Family	Day 1	Day 2	Day 4	Day 6
Jones	52	49	41	34
Sanford	76	64	48	36
Minto	34	32	26	24

1. Graph the water supply data for all three families on the same set of axes. (Colored pens or pencils might help.)

2. Based on this information, who do you think will make it and who will not? Explain your reasoning.

3. Is there a time when all three families will have about the same amount of water left? If so, when?

Note: If any member of one of your group's families has a last name from this assignment, then that family took Sublette's Cutoff and may have saved some time. More to come on this!

Who Will Make It?

Mathematical Topics

• Making predictions based on graphs of data

Outline of the Day

In Class

1. Discuss *Homework 16: Sublette's Cutoff*
   • Make adjustments in travel time for some students' Overland Trail families

2. *Who Will Make It?*
   • Students analyze data about travel progress and make predictions about what will happen to each family

• The activity will be discussed on Day 18

At Home

Homework 17: The Basic Student Budget

1. Discussion of Homework 16: Sublette's Cutoff

Choose two or three groups to give presentations, and give them pens and overhead transparencies to use in their preparations. While they are preparing, other groups should compare answers, and you can check to see who attempted to do the homework.

When groups are ready, have the club card students make the presentations.

Homework 16: Sublette's Cutoff is similar to *Previous Travelers*. However, while students worked with each supply item separately and were told to use linear approximations in *Previous Travelers*, *Homework 16: Sublette's Cutoff* required students to compare the situations of the three families and did not specify a linear approach.

There are many directions that the presentations can take. For example:

- Some groups may assume a linear model for water use, while others may not. Groups that used a nonlinear approach should be asked to explain their method.

- Some groups may have set up their horizontal scales to extend to Day 15, while others may have computed a per-day usage amount and calculated from this what would remain by Day 15. Either of these approaches is fine.

If students bring up the unreliability of using the given data to make a prediction, you can have the class discuss the issue. Perhaps a student will make the point that people often need to make decisions when they do not have all the data, and that an educated guess is better than a random decision.

Check to see that students have set up their scales appropriately. One error that may occur is for students to mark Day 1, Day 2, Day 4, and Day 6 at equal intervals on the horizontal axis, forgetting to take into account the fact that the time intervals are not all the same. (You can refer back to the discussion of Question 2 of *Homework 12: The Issues Involved*.)

Students might want to consider how long someone can go without water in dry conditions and while exerting great amounts of energy. Others may suggest that the three families should share water with each other once one family's water supply runs out.

Encourage this sort of real-life check on the data. It is important for students to see that mathematics is a tool that can *help* them answer these questions, but that it does not necessarily tell the whole story.

• *Impact on students' Overland Trail families*

If any Overland Trail families used the names Jones or Minto, those families will have saved time by using the cutoff, covering the distance in 15 days.

But if any Overland Trail families used the name Sanford, tell them that they ran out of water, got ill, and finally got help from Native Americans in the area. Tell them that this family had to spend an extra 10 days resting and recovering, so the cutoff took them 25 days instead of 15.

These adjustments should apply if anyone in the Overland Trail "family," including a hired hand, has the last name Jones, Minto, or Sanford.

These details will be used by students in their analysis of how long their trip from Fort Laramie to the end of Sublette's Cutoff has taken.

(See the section "From Fort Laramie to the End of Sublette's Cutoff" at the end of Day 18.)

In *Homework 19: What We Needed*, they will find out how long the rest of the trip to Fort Hall will take and whether the supplies they ended up with after *Previous Travelers* were sufficient to make it to Fort Hall.

Note: Students will use graphing calculators to revisit *Homework 16: Sublette's Cutoff* (along with *Homework 18: Out of Action*) on Day 21.

2. *Who Will Make It?*

(see next page)

The problem is quite similar to *Homework 16: Sublette's Cutoff*, so you can just let students get started and see what happens.

All the groups may not finish. Those that do finish can be given pens and overhead transparencies to prepare presentations for tomorrow, when the activity will be discussed. Students in groups that have not finished should complete *Who Will Make It?* tonight (in addition to doing *Homework 17: The Basic Student Budget*).

Students prepare a graph presentation of "Who Will Make It?"

Who Will Make It?

Dagny Appel bought an almanac at the trading post in Fort Laramie. The almanac included predictions about the weather, crops, and livestock.

Dagny was a tireless planner. She shared the predictions with almost everyone in her wagon train. Other wagon trains also became concerned.

One particular prediction worried Dagny: The Green River, some 330 miles away, was expected to flood in 30 days, which was about how long it might take to get there.

Three wagon trains kept track of their distances remaining from the Green River. The table on the next page shows how far each wagon train still was from the river at the end of three different days.

Continued on next page

Distance to the River (in miles)

Wagon train	Day 4	Day 7	Day 11
Fowler	270	235	185
Belshaw	285	260	230
Clappe	280	245	200

Graph the data for all three wagon trains *on the same set of axes.* (Colored pens or pencils might help.)

Then answer these questions.

1. If the almanac is correct about when the flood will take place, who will make it to the Green River before the flood and who will not? Explain your reasoning.

2. If the almanac is wrong and all three groups make it past the river, which wagon train do you think will arrive at the river first? Last? Explain your reasoning.

3. When the first of these wagon trains gets to the Green River, how far back is the next wagon train? What about the last wagon train? Explain how you found your answer.

Note: If any member of one of your group's families had a last name from this assignment, then you should use the data above to figure out how long it took them to get from Fort Laramie to the Green River, and record this time.

Homework 17 The Basic Student Budget

Cal, Bernie, and Doc are college students on basic student budgets.

Sometimes the three have a little difficulty keeping to their budgets. Their biggest problem is the rent.

The total rent for their apartment is $450, which is split evenly among the three roommates. The rent is due on the last day of each month, and the guys don't get paid until the first day of the next month.

Their landlord has no tolerance for late payments.

Continued on next page

Homework 17:
The Basic Student
Budget

This assignment puts the prediction process used in *Homework 16: Sublette's Cutoff* and *Who Will Make It?* into a modern-day context.

• •

Each of the three students had a different amount of money after being paid on April 1. At the end of that day, Cal had $550, Bernie had $400, and Doc had $300. As the month goes by, they each make note occasionally of how much they have left at the end of the day.

The table shows their records so far.

Amount of Money Remaining (in dollars)

Date	Cal	Bernie	Doc
April 3	498	383	285
April 10	352	349	245
April 17	220	313	215

1. Sketch and label a graph that accurately represents this situation. (Show all three students *on the same graph*.)

2. Who will be able to pay his rent on time and who will not? How do you know?

3. It's April 21, and there's a great concert on campus. This would be an extra cost, beyond the three students' normal expenses. How much, if anything, can each one spend and still have enough for rent money on April 30?

4. Suppose each of them starts May with the same amount with which he started April.

    Find an approximate rule for each roommate that will tell him how much money he should expect to have at the end of the *x*th day of May if his spending habits don't change.

To the End of Sublette's Cutoff

Students use their results from recent activities to figure the time their Overland Trail families spent on one leg of the journey.

Mathematical Topics

- Making predictions based on graphs of data
- Finding algebraic expressions for linear approximations of data

Outline of the Day

In Class

1. Discuss *Homework 17: The Basic Student Budget*
   - Use intuitive approaches to find the amount each roommate spends per day
   - Emphasize that the rules will only be approximate, because no straight line fits the data perfectly

2. Discuss *Who Will Make It?* (from Day 17)
   - Try to reach a consensus on how long each family would take to reach the Green River

3. Determine the time it takes for each group to travel from Fort Laramie to the end of Sublette's Cutoff
   - Use data from *Homework 16: Sublette's Cutoff* and *Who Will Make It?* for families with names used in those activities
   - Have students save this information for use in *Homework 19: What We Needed*

At Home

Homework 18: Out of Action

Note: Tomorrow, you'll introduce students to graphing on a graphing calculator. You may want to work with a small group of students ahead of time to facilitate tomorrow's work.

1. Discussion of *Homework 17: The Basic Student Budget*

"How did you find rules for the amount of money each person would have?"

Questions 1 and 2 of this assignment are similar to the prediction process used in *Homework 16: Sublette's Cutoff* and in *Who Will Make It?*

Focus attention in this discussion on Question 4—finding rules for Cal, Bernie, and Doc. This is more complicated than finding rules for many previous In-Out tables because no linear function fits the data perfectly.

Although the data in *Previous Travelers* did not form a linear function, students found a rule for the line of best fit. *In Homework 16: Sublette's Cutoff and Who Will Make It?*, they did not find rules for the data.

You may want to make sure that students took into account the various starting amounts as well as the amounts in the table. In other words, they have four data points—not just three—for each roommate. For example, the information for Cal should also include the amount of $550 for April 1, as well as the amounts for April 3, 10, and 17.

If students had difficulty with this assignment, you may want to go over one example and let them work in groups on the other two. One useful approach is to estimate the daily amount Cal, Bernie, and Doc each spend, and work from there.

You will probably want to talk about how one makes such an estimate, because there are many ways to do it. One good approach would be to take the amount an individual had left at the end of April 17, subtract this from the amount with which he started the month, and divide the difference by 17 (the number of days from the beginning of April 1 to the end of April 17).

But other approaches are possible, including methods that rely more on the graph and less on the table.

Once students have such an estimate, they should be in a good position to find a rule. Essentially what they need to do is to repeatedly subtract the amount the person uses each day from his starting amount. The value of x tells you how many times you need to subtract the daily spending amount. The formula that results is something like this:

amount on day x = initial amount − (amount spent daily) · x

Keep in mind that "amount spent daily" is just an estimate or average, since it is not exactly the same every day.

2. Discussion of *Who Will Make It?*

The discussion of *Who Will Make It?* should pretty much follow the same lines as that for *Homework 16: Sublette's Cutoff.*

Have the groups with prepared transparencies give their presentations to the class while others ask questions and add to the discussion.

If students used the total distance traveled for the first 11 days to find a daily average for each wagon train, then they should have found that the Fowler group took about 25 days, the Belshaw group about 36 days, and the Clappe group about 28 days.

For example, the Fowler group traveled 330 − 185 = 145 miles in 11 days, for an average of about 13.2 miles per day. At this rate, it would take 330 ÷ 13.2 ≈ 25 days to make the 330-mile trip to the Green River.

Because the Belshaw group arrives after the river has flooded, they should add another two days of travel time, for a total of 38 days until they get across the Green River.

Note: If your class reaches a consensus on different values for each family that you think are reasonable, you can use those values instead.

3. From Fort Laramie to the End of Sublette's Cutoff

Next, students need to record the amount of time for their journey from Fort Laramie to the end of Sublette's Cutoff.

Tell students that it took a typical wagon train on the main route 30 days to travel from Fort Laramie to the Green River and 18 days to travel from the Green River to the end of Sublette's Cutoff, for a total of 48 days. Most groups should use this as the value they record.

But groups with families using certain last names will need to make the adjustments described below. (As noted earlier, these adjustments are made if anyone in the Overland Trail "family," including a hired hand, has one of the last names listed.)

Students must save this information for use in *Homework 19: What We Needed,* in which they will find out how long it took to complete the trip to Fort Hall.

• *Special cases*

If groups had families with certain last names, they will need to use different values for the time from Fort Laramie to the end of Sublette's Cutoff, as shown below.

- Fowler: 43 days

- Belshaw: 56 days

- Clappe: 46 days

- Jones or Minto: 41 days

- Sanford: 51 days

If a group used more than one of these family names, then they should record the slowest time of their four families (because they had to wait for the slowest family).

Here are the details.

For families whose names appear in *Who Will Make It?*, students should use the times developed in today's discussion of the activity. If you use the values given in this text, you will have the travel times given below.

- Fowler: 25 days to the Green River plus 18 days from the Green River to the end of Sublette's Cutoff, for a total of 43 days.

- Belshaw: 36 days to the Green River plus 2 days for the flood plus 18 days from the Green River to the end of Sublette's Cutoff, for a total of 56 days.

- Clappe: 28 days to the Green River plus 18 days from the Green River to the end of Sublette's Cutoff, for a total of 46 days.

For families whose names appear in *Homework 16: Sublette's Cutoff,* students should use the travel times below.

- Jones or Minto: 26 days to the beginning of the cutoff plus 15 days for the cutoff itself, for a total of 41 days.

- Sanford: 26 days to the beginning of the cutoff plus 25 days for the cutoff itself, for a total of 51 days.

Homework 18   Out of Action

The general manager of the Slamajamas basketball team has a difficult decision to make.

A key player, Marcus Dunkalot, suffered a sprained knee on March 20, about one month prior to the beginning of the playoffs, and was put on the disabled list.

It is now just over two weeks later, April 6. The general manager needs to decide immediately whether or not to keep Marcus on the disabled list. If he keeps Marcus on the disabled list, it will be for the remainder of the regular season, which means that Marcus will be disqualified for the playoffs.

Here are the advantages and disadvantages of each choice.

- If he takes Marcus off the disabled list now, he can hope that Marcus will be well in time for the playoffs. But if Marcus is not ready in time, then the Slamajamas will have one less player available for the rest of the season, including the playoffs.

- If he keeps Marcus on the disabled list, he can sign another player (of lesser ability) to take his place. But then he gives up all hope of having Marcus for the playoffs.

The playoffs begin on April 18.

On the next page is a copy of the physical therapist's report, on which the general manager must base his immediate decision.

Continued on next page

Homework 18: Out of Action

Tonight's homework is similar to *Homework 17: Basic Student Budget,* although students will need to do some work to identify the key information.

PROFESSIONAL PHYSICAL THERAPY

Patient's name: Marcus Dunkalot

Sex: male   Height: 6'8"

Age: 24   Weight: 225 lbs.

Diagnosis: sprained knee

Prescribed treatment: strengthen and stretch

3/20   Mr. Dunkalot was administered a Cybex strength test upon arrival. Quadriceps of the injured leg measured 55 foot-pounds in extension. Normal measurement for a player to return to play without reinjury is 250 foot-pounds.

3/25   Daily regimen is contributing to patient's progress. Cybex test measures 90 foot-pounds.

4/1   Some swelling earlier in the week. General reports of less pain. Cybex test measures 140 foot-pounds.

4/6   Less swelling. Range of motion has shown marked increase. Cybex test measures 185 foot-pounds.

1. Graph Marcus Dunkalot's progress.

2. Imagine that you are the general manager. The team owners want a complete report on why and how you made your decision. What will you decide? Write the report.

Days 19-25

Calculators on the Trail?

This page in the student book introduces Days 19 through 25.

You've got a big advantage over the folks on the Overland Trail—you get to use a graphing calculator in your work. As you reach Fort Hall and then move on toward California, you'll see how to use the calculator to make graphs and you'll use calculator graphs to look back at some problems you've already worked on.

Brian Jones explains his work from "Fair Share on Chores" to Judy Kodotan, parent of a prospective student.

You've already seen that every equation has a graph. In one new type of problem, you'll look at how graphs can help you find a solution when you have two equations in a single situation.

Calculator In-Outs

Students learn to graph functions on their graphing calculators.

Mathematical Topics

- Finding algebraic expressions for linear approximations of data
- Graphing on a graphing calculator

Outline of the Day

In Class

1. Get a progress report on students' work on *POW 10: On Your Own*

2. Discuss *Homework 18: Out of Action*

3. Introduce graphing of functions on graphing calculators, including the following operations:

   - Entering and editing functions
   - Adjusting the viewing rectangle, directly or by using the zoom feature
   - Using the trace feature
   - Getting a table of values

4. *Graphing Calculator In-Outs*

   - Students graph equations and use the graphs to answer questions

- The activity will be completed and discussed on Day 20

5. Get students to assemble the following information for *Homework 19: What We Needed:*

   - The number of people in each of their group's four Overland Trail families
   - The travel time from Fort Laramie to the end of Sublette's Cutoff (from Day 18)
   - The rate of travel from the end of Sublette's Cutoff to Fort Hall (by rolling dice)

At Home

Homework 19: What We Needed

Special Materials Needed

- An overhead projector for use with the graphing calculator
- Dice (two per group)

1. Progress Report on *POW 10: On Your Own*

"How are you doing on your POW?"

Ask how students are doing on their current POW. Since this is a different kind of assignment, they may need some guidance as to how to go about it. Perhaps they can give each other advice about where to get information.

2. Discussion of *Homework 18: Out of Action*

Let students report on their results from the assignment.

The homework has at least two elements that distinguish it from most of the recent prediction problems.

- Students need to work to extract most of the information from the problem. In earlier assignments (*Homework 16: Sublette's Cutoff; Who Will Make It?;* and *Homework 17: The Basic Student Budget*), the data was presented in a table.

- There is no particular reason to assume that the graphed data will have a linear form. In the three problems just listed, linearity was a natural assumption.

Note: In *Homework 15: Broken Promises,* students had to find the data by estimating areas, and there was no particular reason in that problem to assume that the graph would be linear.

Some students may have gone astray working with the calendar, perhaps forgetting that March has 31 days, or getting confused about whether to treat March 20 as Day 0 or Day 1. If they treat March 20 as Day 1, then the numbering of the important dates should be

- March 25: Day 6
- April 1: Day 13
- April 6: Day 18
- April 18: Day 30

Note: Some students may treat March 20 as Day 20, in which case April 1 becomes Day 32, and so on. This method is perfectly correct, but will lead to a different set of data points for graphing on this unit's Day 21.

As mentioned on Day 17, students will be revisiting both *Homework 18: Out of Action* and *Homework 16: Sublette's Cutoff* on Day 21, and will be using the graphing calculator.

3. Graphing on a Calculator

Today's main goal is for students to get acquainted with the basic elements of graphing functions on their graphing calculators. They should learn how to do the operations listed below.

- Enter and edit functions and have the calculator draw their graphs.

- Adjust the **viewing rectangle**, either directly or by using a **zoom** feature, to see a particular portion of the graph and get more precise information about the graph.

- Use the **trace** feature to get the coordinates of a point on a graph from the calculator.

- (Optional) Get a table of values on the calculator.

Note: Some students may have discovered a few of these operations on their own, but you should probably assume that most of them have no experience with the graphing capabilities of their calculators.

You can begin the work on graphing by illustrating the procedures with one or two simple examples, starting with linear functions, such as $y = 2x + 5$. Then let students explore for a little while on their own.

One point to emphasize is that the calculator will only graph an equation that is entered in the "$Y=$" form, that is, which expresses the output, which the calculator calls Y, directly in terms of the input, which the calculator calls X.

4. Graphing Calculator In-Outs

(see next page)

When students seem to be comfortable with the simple mechanics of operation, have them begin work on *Calculator In-Outs*. (You may want to lead the class as a whole through the work on Question 1.)

Help them to understand the need to zoom or to adjust the viewing rectangle to get the right part of the graph on the screen. Finding a good range is an essential skill for working with graphing calculators. Encourage students to play with the range and to develop their own strategies. This will allow students to gain confidence in themselves and to stop looking for rules or "the right way."

The activity will be completed tomorrow.

Graphing Calculator In-Outs

Some of the things you have been doing with pencil-and-paper graphs can also be done on a graphing calculator.

You will probably decide that some problems are easier to do on the graphing calculator than on paper, and others are easier to do on paper. This activity will help you get used to the new method.

Continued on next page

Keep in mind that you may often have to adjust the viewing window for your graphing screen. You may find this easiest to do by using the zoom feature of the graphing calculator.

1. In the activity *Previous Travelers,* you found a rule for estimating the number of pounds of beans needed for different numbers of people making the trip from Fort Laramie to Fort Hall.

   Although you may have found a different rule in that activity, you should now use the function listed here.

   Number of pounds of beans = 12 · (number of people)

   a. Enter and graph this function on a graphing calculator.

   Now use the trace feature on your graphing calculator to answer the questions below.

   b. How many pounds of beans are needed for 20 people?

   c. A certain family brought 155 pounds of beans. According to the function above, how many people can they feed?

2. In *Homework 8: To Kearny by Equation,* you were given an equation for the profit that Joseph and Lewis Papan each made from their ferry service. That equation depended in part on how many hours the captain worked.

   But suppose the Papans decide to pay the captain for ten hours of work each day, regardless of the amount of business.

   In that case, the profit each gets for a given day could be determined by the equation below (in which W is the number of wagons that the ferry captain takes across the river).

   $$\text{profit} = \frac{W - 4}{2}$$

   a. Enter and graph this function on your graphing calculator.

   Now use the trace feature on your graphing calculator to answer the questions below.

   b. How much profit will the Papans each make if 25 wagons use their ferry?

   c. How many wagons will have to use the Papans' ferry for the Papans to make $15 each?

Continued on next page

3. The In-Out table shown here is for the function

$$Y = 3X^2 - 7X + 2$$

Graph this function on your graphing calculator and use the zoom and trace features to find the missing entries.

Where the *Out* value is given, find all possible *In* values that will give the desired *Out*. If there aren't any, write "none."

Give your answers to the nearest tenth.

In	Out
1.31	?
-3.02	?
?	-1.04
?	-2.12
?	-2.05
8.57	?

5. Getting Ready for *Homework 19: What We Needed*

(see next page)

Near the end of class today, you will need to prepare students for tonight's homework assignment.

They will need to know how long it took them to go from Fort Laramie to the end of Sublette's Cutoff.

If you didn't go over this information yesterday, be sure to leave time to do it now. If you are using the figures in this text, the travel time is 48 days, except for the special families, whose travel times are shown below.

- Fowler: 43 days

- Belshaw: 56 days

- Clappe: 46 days

- Jones or Minto: 41 days

- Sanford: 51 days

Each group needs to roll a pair of dice and add the sum to 8, to represent the average number of miles per day that they travel from the end of Sublette's Cutoff to Fort Hall. (This will give a range of from 10 to 20 miles per day.)

Tomorrow, groups will match the amounts to be found in Questions 3 and 4 of this assignment with the amounts they brought from *Previous Travelers,* to see if their supplies lasted.

Homework 19   What We Needed

Part I: Traveling Time

In the first part of this assignment, you will figure out how long it took for your group's families to travel the entire distance from Fort Laramie to Fort Hall.

1. You should already know how many days it took for your group's families to go from Fort Laramie to the end of Sublette's Cutoff.

   Write down this time.

2. Next, you need to find out how long it took your group's families to go from the end of Sublette's Cutoff to Fort Hall.

   You should have rolled a pair of dice, found the sum, and added that to 8. Use this result to represent the average rate (in miles per day) at which your

Continued on next page

families traveled for this portion of the trip, which is a distance of 120 miles. (You should have a rate between 10 miles per day and 20 miles per day.)

Based on this rate, find out how many days it took from the end of Sublette's Cutoff to Fort Hall.

3. Add the results from Questions 1 and 2 to get the total number of days it took for your families to get from Fort Laramie to Fort Hall.

Part II: Supplies Needed

4. It turns out that each person in your group's families ate an average of 0.22 pounds of beans per day between Fort Laramie and Fort Hall. Calculate the amount of beans each of your group's four families needed to bring on the trip.

5. It also turns out that each person used an average of 0.08 pounds of sugar per day. Find the amount of sugar that each of your group's families needed to bring.

DAY 20 More Calculator In-Outs

Students continue to work with graphing calculators.

Mathematical Topics

- Graphing, zooming, and tracing on a graphing calculator

Outline of the Day

In Class

1. Discuss *Homework 19: What We Needed*
   - Calculate the loss of life in Overland Trail families
2. Complete and discuss *Graphing Calculator In-Outs* (from Day 19)

- Groups can make presentations on individual problems

At Home

Homework 20: More Graph Sketches

Special Materials Needed

- An overhead projector for use with the graphing calculator

1. Discussion of Homework 19: What We Needed

Rather than bring the whole class together, you may want to have students share their results on the homework assignment within their groups.

You can have students compare calculations from last night's homework to be sure all the members of a group got the same answers for Part I. Circulate among the groups to confirm that they are doing this properly.

For your convenience: Unless their families had one or more of the special names, groups will use 48 days for Question 1, as noted at the end of Day 18. For Question 2, students should compute $120/n$, where n is the number they obtained yesterday by adding 8 to the sum of a rolled pair of dice.

They should then compare the quantities they found they needed (in Part II) with the quantities they brought on this leg of the trip, as recorded following the discussion of *Previous Travelers*.

• *Death on the trail*

After groups have shared results, bring the class together to talk about the consequences of their results.

Overland Trail families that did not take the warning in *Previous Travelers* seriously may have ended up short of supplies. Bad luck between the end of Sublette's Cutoff and Fort Hall (that is, a low roll of the dice yesterday) could also account for problems.

You can tell students that families that were short of supplies had to bury people on the trail. You might use a simple scheme and say that groups that did not have enough supplies lost 10 percent of their family members.

Groups should record any deaths in their folders.

If you want the losses to depend on how far off students were from what they needed, here is a scheme you can use.

- Find the smaller percentage shortfall of the two commodities, beans and sugar.

- Count as dead that percentage of the given family (rounded down).

For example, if a given Overland Trail family had 85% of the beans it needed and 92% of the sugar it needed, then they were short 15% and 8% respectively, and they should

use the 8% figure. Then, for example, if the family has 19 members, they find 8% of 19, which is 1.52, and must bury one person.

Note: The per-person amounts given in Part II of the homework were chosen with the *Previous Travelers* data and the travel time information in mind, so that groups who followed the directions and did the mathematics carefully should generally not lose any family members. Exceptions may occur due to very low dice rolls in *Homework 19: What We Needed.*

2. Completion of *Graphing Calculator In-Outs*

Groups should complete their work on this activity.

Assign a problem from *Calculator In-Outs* to each of the first three groups finished, and ask them to prepare a presentation. (If you did Question 1 as a whole class, you will probably skip having a presentation on that.)

There is really not much for groups to share, other than to check that there was a consensus on the answers. All students should be getting better at

manipulating viewing rectangles and using other techniques for calculator graphing as a result of their work on these problems.

Homework 20   More Graph Sketches

Do you remember graph sketches? For each of the situations below, sketch a graph that might represent what is happening.

Include an appropriate scale on each of your axes.

1. The length of a burning candle as a function of the amount of time the candle has been burning.

2. The weight of a person as a function of that person's age, over the course of a lifetime.

3. The distance left to California as a function of the length of time since the wagon train left Westport.

4. The height off the ground of a buffalo chip stuck to a wagon wheel as a function of time (over three revolutions of the wheel).

5. Make up a situation of your own and sketch a graph.

*Homework 20:
More Graph
Sketches*

This assignment is a review of graph sketches, introduced on Day 11.

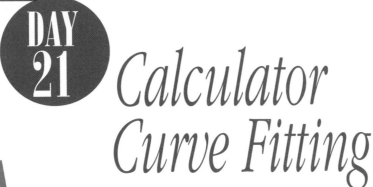

Calculator Curve Fitting

Mathematical Topics

- Plotting data with the graphing calculator
- Looking for a function that approximates the given data

Outline of the Day

In Class

1. Discuss *Homework 20: More Graph Sketches*
2. Introduce curve fitting on the graphing calculator, including
   - Entering and plotting data points
   - Using a guess-and-check approach to finding a curve that fits the data
3. *"Out of Action" and "Sublette's Cutoff" Revisited*
   - Students reexamine the situations described in these

activities and use the graphing calculator and curve-fitting techniques to answer questions
   - No whole-class discussion of this activity is needed

At Home

Homework 21: Biddy Mason

- Students will need to know the number of people in the Overland Trail family for which they are responsible

Discuss With Your Colleagues

Who's the Calculator Expert?

Graphing calculators were not part of our own educational experience, and many teachers feel outclassed by their students in working with this new technology. How can you take advantage of the fact that some of your students may be more comfortable with the graphing calculator than you are?

1. Discussion of *Homework 20: More Graph Sketches*

Students can share their graph sketches in their groups. If you notice any common misconceptions or difficulties, you may want to bring them to the attention of the entire class.

You may also want to have several students share the situations they made up and the sketches they made to represent those situations.

2. Calculator Curve Fitting

Today's main activity is to reexamine *Homework 18: Out of Action* and *Homework 16: Sublette's Cutoff,* using the graphing calculator as an aid to curve fitting.

You will need to demonstrate how to enter and plot data points on the calculator. You can use data from one of the families from *Who Will Make It?* for this demonstration.

"How can you get a good function for these data points?"

Once students see how to enter and plot points, you might let them discuss how to proceed to get a good function for the *Who Will Make It?* data. The basic curve-fitting technique is as follows:

- Plot the data on the graphing calculator.

- Leave the data on the screen and graph a function that you think might approximate the data well.

- Examine how closely your function's graph approximates the data, and adjust the function until you think it approximates the data as well as possible.

Note: In *Homework 18: Out of Action* and *Homework 16: Sublette's Cutoff,* students were asked to give only yes-or-no answers to questions about their graphs, and were not asked to find equations of functions to fit the data.

In *Homework 18: Out of Action,* the question was, "Will Marcus Dunkalot's leg strength reach 250 foot-pounds by April 18?" In *Homework 16: Sublette's Cutoff,* the question was, "Will the given family have enough water for 15 days?" The questions in this assignment are somewhat different.

"Out of Action" and "Sublette's Cutoff" Revisited

In both *Homework 18: Out of Action* and *Homework 16: Sublette's Cutoff*, you were given certain data about a situation, and asked to make a prediction.

In both problems, you plotted the data and based your prediction on a pencil-and-paper graph.

Now, you are to reexamine those two situations, answering a slightly different question for each and using a different technique.

Here is the technique you will use.

- Plot the data on a graphing calculator.

- Leave the data on the screen and graph a function that you think might approximate the data well.

- Examine how closely your function's graph approximates the data, and adjust the function until you think it approximates the data as well as possible.

- Use your final choice of function to make a prediction.

Continued on next page

3. "Out of Action" and "Sublette's Cutoff" Revisited

After you have introduced the calculator operations and the broad outline of the approach, let students work in groups on *"Out of Action" and "Sublette's Cutoff" Revisited.*

1. "Out of Action" Revisited

In *Homework 18: Out of Action,* you were given data about a basketball player's leg strength. The information from that problem is given below.

- March 20   55 foot-pounds

- March 25   90 foot-pounds

- April 1   140 foot-pounds

- April 6   185 foot-pounds

Use the technique described above to predict what Marcus Dunkalot's leg strength will be on April 18.

2. "Sublette's Cutoff" Revisited

In *Homework 16: Sublette's Cutoff,* you were given data showing the amount of water each of three families had at the end of certain days. The information from that problem is reproduced in this table.

Gallons of Water Remaining

Family	Day 1	Day 2	Day 4	Day 6
Jones	52	49	41	34
Sanford	76	64	48	36
Minto	34	32	26	24

Use the technique described above to predict how much water each family would have at the end of Day 15. You will probably want to do one family at a time.

(If you think a family would run out of water before Day 15, then you will give a negative prediction here.)

There is no formal discussion scheduled for this activity, and no discussion suggestions are provided here. You can probably get a sense of whether discussion as a whole class is needed by observing the groups.

It is not necessary for students to finish all parts of the activity. The calculator experience that the activity provides is not needed for tonight's homework.

Homework 21   Biddy Mason

Hundreds of thousands of people traveled to California in the middle of the nineteenth century.

Some came across the Pacific Ocean from China. Some sailed from the Atlantic coast to Panama, crossed land there, and then sailed again to California.

Still others, as you know, came by boat around Cape Horn or came by wagon or by horse on the Overland Trail.

Biddy Mason walked.

About Biddy Mason

Biddy Mason walked to California behind her master's 300-wagon train. Her job was to watch the cattle, but her master would not give her a horse, so she had to walk. She was one of the uncounted number of enslaved African Americans brought to California by southern slave owners to work in the gold fields.

Continued on next page

Homework 21: Biddy Mason

Tonight's homework combines the search for functions to describe situations with a poignant story taken from the time of the Overland Trail.

• •

Biddy Mason broke away from her slave master and had the courage to sue for and win her freedom. She settled in California, where she became known for her generosity and great charity, taking in homeless children and supporting schools, churches, and hospitals.

Most enslaved people, however, were not able to win their freedom as Biddy Mason did.

Your Problem

Suppose that shortly after you leave Fort Hall, your Overland Trail family encounters a family that has escaped from slavery.

You need to think about whether to let them join your group. Since they have no supplies of their own, you would need to share what you have with them.

1. Pick one of your supply items, and decide how much of that item you have at the time you meet this family. (Pick an amount that seems reasonable as a total for about 20 days.)

   a. Write down your total amount of this supply item and the number of people in your Overland Trail family.

   b. Figure out how much of the supply item there is per person (for your Overland Trail family).

2. a. Suppose that the family you meet consists of four people. If you let them join you, how much of the supply item will there be per person? (Assume that everyone gets an equal share.)

   b. What if the family you meet has six people?

3. Find an equation that gives the amount you will have for each person as a function of the number of people in the family you meet.

4. Graph the function from Question 3. Choose scales for your axes that are appropriate to the information you are considering.

Fair Share on Chores

Students represent a situation with a linear equation and solve the equation for one variable in terms of the other.

Mathematical Topics

- Solving equations for one variable in terms of the other
- Graphing linear conditions
- Using graphing calculators to get information

Outline of the Day

In Class

1. Discuss *Homework 21: Biddy Mason*
   - Use arithmetic steps in Questions 1 and 2 to develop an algebraic expression for Question 3

2. *Fair Share on Chores*
   - Students represent a situation by using a linear equation
   - Students use the pattern of numerical examples to solve the equation for one variable in terms of the other
   - Students graph the new form of the equation on a graphing calculator and use the graph to find more solutions

3. Discuss *Fair Share on Chores*
   - Emphasize the connection between the graph and the equation: Points that fit the equation lie on the graph, and vice versa
   - Post the equation from Question 4 for use in *More "Fair Share on Chores"* (Day 23)

At Home

Homework 22: *Fair Share for Hired Hands*

1. Discussion of *Homework 21: Biddy Mason*

You may want to have at least two spade card students make presentations on the homework, since they will probably use different initial amounts per person and will also have different family sizes.

If students had trouble finding a rule, ask, "How did you get the answers for Question 2?"

If students had difficulty finding a function rule (in Question 3), help them work through the arithmetic of individual cases in Question 2, focusing on where the numbers come from.

For example, suppose they started with 40 pounds of beans and an Overland Trail family of nine people. They should then get $40/9 \approx 6.7$ pounds per person for Question 1b.

In Question 2a, if they let a family of four join them, there will be $40/13 \approx 3.1$ pounds per person. Help students see that the denominator of 13 is the result of adding 4 to the original family size of 9. Using this example as a model, and perhaps also looking at their work on Question 2b, they should see that, in general, the amount per person is given by the equation $y = \frac{40}{9+n}$, in which n is the number of people that join their Overland Trail family.

You can bring out that in the context of the problem, it only makes sense to use this equation for positive integer values of n. But the equation itself makes sense for arbitrary numbers, including negative values for n.

Ask students to enter their functions on their graphing calculators. Be sure students notice that the graph of such a function is not linear (if this hasn't already come up in the discussion).

"What happens if you change the viewing rectangle?"

You can have them try different viewing rectangles. They may notice that the graph is displaying behavior that they may consider bizarre. Use your judgment about how much to get into this issue. (The concept of asymptotic behavior is considered in a Year 4 unit, *The World of Functions*.)

Students can also compare how the graphs change with different initial quantities of a supply item.

2. *Fair Share on Chores*

(see next page)

Two important concepts will be reinforced in today's activity, *Fair Share on Chores*.

- Abstracting a problem to an algebraic equation
- Reading specific numerical information from a graph

Let students work for a while in groups on *Fair Share on Chores*.

You may want to have a student find a sample solution for Question 1 as a way to get the whole class started. Also, you may need to prompt students to consider values other than whole numbers in Question 1.

In Question 2, students are asked to express a problem condition by using an equation. Although this task may seem straightforward, translating words into symbols is a complex process. Using variables as called for in this question builds on the earlier work in the unit on the meaningful use of variables (such as that in *Ox Expressions*).

As a hint, you can ask,

"If each girl's shift was four hours, how would you find the length of each boy's shift?"

Some students may have trouble with Questions 3 and 4. Other students might be able to help them, or you can ask a specific question, such as "If each girl's shift was four hours, what is the process you would go through to find the length of each boy's shift?"

Students may answer Question 3 with a sentence like this: "Double the length of each girl's shift, subtract that from ten, and then divide what's left by three." They may need help in expressing their statement as an equation like $B = \frac{10-2G}{3}$.

When most groups are finished, bring the class together for a discussion.

Fair Share on Chores

About 50 miles past Fort Hall, the California Trail splits from the Oregon Trail and heads into Nevada.

Two families, the Murphys and the Bensons, have decided to continue on the Oregon Trail, and you say good-bye to them as you head for California.

Wagon trains often put their wagons in a circle to make a corral for the livestock. (It was only in the movies that wagon trains created a circle to protect themselves from Native Americans.)

Now that the Murphys and the Bensons have split from the wagon train, you have fewer wagons available.

Continued on next page

The Washburn family decides that someone needs to keep an eye on their animals during the night, and that their children will take shifts each night, with one child at a time guarding the animals. Altogether, the animals need to be watched for ten hours. This family has two girls and three boys.

This sounds simple—two hours each. But the girls have other chores, and so do the boys. In order to balance out other assigned chores, the Washburn family decides that there should be one length of time for each girl's shift and another length of time for each boy's shift.

1. How long would you suggest that *each type* of shift be? Provide at least three different pairs of answers.

2. Using G to represent the length of each girl's shift and B to represent the length of each boy's shift, write an equation expressing the fact that the total of all their shifts is ten hours.

3. Now suppose you know how long each girl's shift is. Describe *in words* how you could find the length of each boy's shift.

4. Write your sentence from Question 3 as a function expressing B in terms of G. That is, write an equation that begins "$B = \ldots$," and has an expression using G on the right of the equal sign.

5. Graph the function from Question 4 on your calculator, and check to see if your answers from Question 1 are on the graph.

6. Use the trace feature on your calculator to find three more pairs of possible shift lengths from your graph.

3. Discussion of *Fair Share on Chores*

Begin the discussion by asking students to compile their possible answers to Question 1 into an In-Out table. Since they are using *G* for the length of each girl's shift, that length should go in the *In* column. Have students plot these points.

"How can you check to see if a number pair fits the condition?"

Then go on to Question 2. If students had trouble with it, ask how they would check to see if a particular number pair fits the condition. They will probably reply by saying something to this effect: "Multiply the length of a girl's shift by two and the length of a boy's shift by three and add." Essentially, they have given you the equation, and they just need to restate it symbolically.

"Why do you want to express one variable in terms of the other?"

Make sure students realize that the purpose of Questions 3 and 4 is to get the equation in a form so they can graph it on the calculator. Otherwise, they could stick with the equation $2G + 3B = 10$, which is probably a more natural way to think about the problem.

Here are some observations that students might make during the discussion.

- The longer the shift for each girl, the shorter the shift for each boy.

- There is a maximum length of shift possible for each group.

- The points that fit the equation lie on a straight line.

- Any point that is on the graph fits the equation, and vice versa.

- There are many different ways to express a relationship.

Post the equation from Question 4 of *Fair Share on Chores* so students can refer to it tomorrow.

Homework 22 Fair Share for Hired Hands

The Fulkerth family is a large one, and they have seven hired hands.

The family has a total of about $20 per week available for salaries.

Four of the hired hands are experienced at working on the trail, and the other three are on their first trip.

It seems fair that the experienced hired hands should get more pay than those without experience. So the Fulkerths decide that there will be two weekly pay rates—one rate for each of the four experienced workers and another rate for each of the three without experience.

1. What should each of the weekly pay rates be? Suggest three possible combinations. (The salary total can be a few cents more or less than $20 if that helps you avoid fractions of a penny.)

2. Plot your three combinations from Question 1, using X for the pay rate of an inexperienced hired hand and Y for the pay rate of an experienced hired hand.

3. Connect the points with a straight line and use this graph to find two more possible pairs.

4. Describe *in words* how you could compute the weekly pay rate for an experienced hired hand if you knew the rate for an inexperienced hired hand.

5. Express your sentence from Question 4 as an equation giving Y in terms of X.

6. Check to see if the two new pairs from Question 3 fit the equation from Question 5.

Homework 22: Fair Share for Hired Hands

This homework problem deals with the same concepts found in the classwork assignment *Fair Share on Chores*.

DAY 23 *Two Equations*

Students discover that solving a problem with two conditions can be done using the intersection of their graphs.

Mathematical Topics

- Combining two linear conditions
- Using the point of intersection of graphs to satisfy two conditions

Outline of the Day

In Class

1. Remind students that *POW 10: On Your Own* is due tomorrow

2. Discuss *Homework 22: Fair Share for Hired Hands*

3. More *"Fair Share on Chores"*
   - Students represent a second condition by using a linear equation, then look for a solution that fits both the new condition and the condition from yesterday's *Fair Share on Chores*

4. Discuss *More "Fair Share on Chores"*
   - If necessary, add a graphical approach to the methods of solution presented by students

At Home

Homework 23: More *"Fair Share for Hired Hands"*

1. POW Presentation Preparation

Tomorrow, *all* students will present their work on *POW 10: On Your Own*, sharing their results within their groups. Remind them that even if they worked with a partner, they each need to do their own write-ups.

2. Discussion of Homework 22: Fair Share for Hired Hands

You can begin by having several heart card students share their solutions for Question 1 of the homework and plot them on the board.

"How did you get Y from X?"

Next, it may be best to go straight to Question 4, getting several verbal descriptions (if there are several) of how to get Y from X, and comparing the different versions.

Then look at the equations students got for Question 5. They probably got something very much like $Y = \frac{20 - 3X}{4}$.

You can then go back to Question 3 and test some of the points students found from their graphs.

• Fitting the equation, being on the graph, and being a solution to the problem

"What is the relationship between fitting the equation and being on the graph?"

The three conditions in the subtitle above—fitting the equation, being on the graph, and being a solution to the problem—are related but distinct. Lead a discussion with the class on how they are related.

You can begin by asking about the relationship between fitting the equation and being on the graph. Students should come to this conclusion:

> *Every point on the graph represents a solution to the equation and every solution to the equation corresponds to a point on the graph.*

Essentially this is the definition of the graph.

"Is every solution to the problem included in the graph?"
"Does every point on the graph represent a solution to the problem?"

Then ask the class whether every solution to the problem is included in the graph, and whether every point on the graph represents a solution to the problem.

The discussion should bring out the fact that a point on the graph (which represents a solution to the equation) does not necessarily represent a solution to the problem.

For example, the point represented by $X = 4$ and $Y = 2$ is on the graph and fits the equation, but it doesn't solve the problem, because the experienced hired hands are supposed to have a higher pay rate than the inexperienced ones.

Even though the graph does represent the equation, the equation itself does not precisely represent the problem. The graph for the actual problem is only a portion of the line. In other problems, only points with whole number coordinates will fit the problem.

• Comparison with "Fair Share on Chores"

Before beginning the next activity, take a few minutes and have the class compare last night's homework with yesterday's classwork, in order to review the equation and graph that students got yesterday. It will help in today's activity, *More "Fair Share on Chores,"* if that equation and graph are fresh in their minds.

3. More "Fair Share on Chores"

(see next page)

Today's activity looks at the task of solving a system of equations, although it does not use that terminology.

It begins with the basic scenario of yesterday's *Fair Share on Chores* activity, but presents a different sort of condition on the two shift lengths.

The work required in Question 1 is similar to yesterday's work.

However, Question 2 adds an additional condition (this is the original condition from yesterday) and asks students to find a solution that works for this second condition as well as for that in Question 1.

Begin by letting students work on *More "Fair Share on Chores"* in their groups. They should not have much trouble with the various parts of Question 1. If they do have difficulty, then you need to work with them (either one group at a time or as a whole class), reviewing their classwork and homework from yesterday.

Once students are clear about Question 1, you should let groups struggle to find their own way to solve Question 2.

Students have several strategies available to them, including these three.

- They can look at the In-Out tables to see if they have any common entries.

- They can graph the two functions on their calculators and use the trace feature to find the coordinates of the point of intersection.

- They can graph just one of the functions and use the trace feature to look for a point on the graph whose coordinates satisfy the other equation.

More Fair Share on Chores

As you saw in *Fair Share for Chores,* the Washburn family's two girls and three boys are responsible for watching the animals in shifts during the night.

After some experience, the family has decided that in order to balance out other chores, the shift for each boy should be half an hour longer than that for each girl.

They have realized, however, that as the season gradually changes, the total amount of time needed for the shifts is not always ten hours. Therefore, they want to know about combinations of shift lengths with different totals.

Continued on next page

Whether students use graphs or tables (or some other approach), there is a major "aha!" involved in the idea of finding a common solution to the two conditions. If students can come up with their own way of putting this process together, the experience will be much more powerful for them. So it's probably best if you can keep your hints to a bare minimum.

When each group has found a solution, pick two or three groups to present their methods to the entire class.

1. a. What are some possible combinations of shift lengths in which the shift for each boy is half an hour longer than that for each girl? Give four possibilities. (Remember that the total time does not need to be ten hours.)

   b. Describe *in words* how you could find the length of each boy's shift if you knew the length of a girl's shift.

   c. Use your answer to Question 1b to write an equation in which *G* represents the length of each girl's shift and *B* represents the length of each boy's shift.

   d. Graph your equation on the calculator.

   e. For each combination that you gave in Question 1a, state how much *total time* will be covered by all the children combined.

2. On a particular evening, it turns out that ten hours of animal watching is required after all.

   Find a pair of shift lengths that would total ten hours and still have the shift for each boy be half an hour longer than the shift for each girl.
   (*Reminder:* There are two girls and three boys. You may want to use your earlier work from *Fair Share on Chores*.)

4. Discussion of *More "Fair Share on Chores"*

You can begin, if you think it is needed, with a discussion of the individual parts of Question 1, or perhaps you can just have a student give the equation from Question 1c. The student will presumably come up with the equation

$$B = G + \frac{1}{2}$$

Then let the chosen groups present their work on Question 2.

If hints are needed, ask:
"How did you represent the first condition graphically?"
"How did you represent the second condition graphically?"
"What points fit both conditions?"

If no group uses a graphical method to solve the system, you can lead the students to a graphical solution by asking a sequence of questions like the one below.

- How did you represent graphically the pairs of shift lengths where each boy's shift is half an hour longer than each girl's shift?

- How did you represent graphically the pairs of shift lengths that total ten hours?

- How can you represent graphically the pairs of shift lengths that fit both conditions?

Students will presumably recognize that each condition by itself is represented graphically by a line. If necessary, emphasize that every point on a given line fits the equation for that line. It shouldn't be hard to get someone to articulate that they want to find a point that is on both lines.

Since students have the equations for both graphs in a form that gives B in terms of G, they can draw the two graphs simultaneously on the screen. The graphs of the two equations look like this.

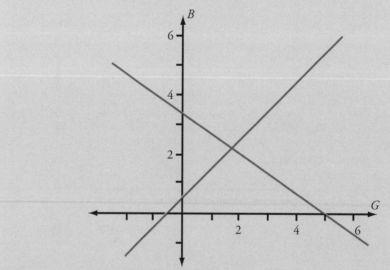

Students can then use the trace feature to estimate the coordinates of the point of intersection. (The point is exactly (1.7, 2.2), which translates to 1 hour, 42 minutes for each girl and 2 hours, 12 minutes for each boy.)

Have students verify that the pair of times represented by the point of intersection actually fits both conditions of the problem.

Homework 23

More Fair Share for Hired Hands

Once again, the Fulkerth family is planning its budget. Times are a little better now, but they haven't yet decided what the total budget should be for hired hands.

The same hired hands are still working for them. So there are now four hired hands who are very experienced and three with only a little experience.

Although all the hired hands have some experience, the Fulkerths decide to continue having two pay rates. In the new pay scale, a very experienced hired hand will get $1 per week more than a less experienced hired hand.

1. Make several suggestions of ways the Fulkerths could set up the two pay rates. Put this data in a table, in which X represents a less experienced worker's weekly pay rate and Y represents a more experienced worker's weekly pay rate.

2. Graph the data from the table, and write an equation for your graph.

3. Find a set of pay rates that would make the total weekly pay for the hired hands approximately $30.

Homework 23:
More Fair Share for Hired Hands

Tonight's homework has the same relationship to last night's homework that today's activity had to yesterday's activity.

In order to encourage students to use a graphing approach, you might suggest that they take home the graph from last night's *Homework 22: Fair Share for Hired Hands*.

POW 10
Presentations

Students share
their
conclusions
from POW 10
with their
group
members.

Mathematical Topics

• More work with pairs of linear conditions

Outline of the Day

In Class

1. Discuss *Homework 23: More "Fair Share for Hired Hands"*

2. Discussions within groups of *POW 10: On Your Own*

At Home

POW 11: High-Low Differences (due Day 29)

Homework 24: Different High-Lows

1. Discussion of Homework 23: More "Fair Share for Hired Hands"

"How did you find the different pay rates?"

Let several students share their ideas for finding the appropriate pay rates.

As before, there are several ways to approach the problem, and students may not have solved the homework by graphing the two equations.

They should have the graph of the equation $Y = X + 1$ for Question 2, but they might have answered Question 3 by a guess-and-check method.

"What equation
represents the
information in
Question 3?"

Ask the groups to come up with an equation that would represent the additional information provided in Question 3.

"How can you
rewrite the equation
3X + 4Y = 30 so you
can graph it on the
graphing calculator?"
(Possible hint: "How
would you find the
rate of pay for each
more experienced
hand if you knew the
rate for each less
experienced hand?")

If they come up with $3X + 4Y = 30$ (which is likely), ask them how they would put this equation in a form that would allow them to graph it on the graphing calculator. You may want to suggest that they think about how they would find the rate for each more experienced hand if they knew the rate for each less experienced hand.

If needed, have them go through the arithmetic with a specific value for X, and then analyze the arithmetic steps (in a manner like that described on Day 22 for *Fair Share on Chores*). They should be able to express the condition that the pay total is $30 in a form similar to $Y = \frac{30 - 3X}{4}$.

For your convenience: The solution is that less experienced hired hands each get about $3.71 per week, while more experienced hired hands each get about $4.71 per week. (This gives a total weekly pay of $29.97 for all the hired hands.)

2. Group Sharing of *POW 10: On Your Own*

Have students share what they learned within their groups.

There is no specific mathematical lesson that needs to come out of these presentations. You may want to have the whole class discuss what they learned from this assignment, both in terms of mathematics and in terms of more general skills.

POW 11: High-Low Differences
(see facing page)

This POW has a different quality from those that students have done before, since it is quite open-ended, with no particular question to be answered.

Students may have difficulty with the lack of structure, but the exploratory nature of this problem represents an important kind of mathematical thinking. Students will have many similar problems over the course of the curriculum. You should take a long-range view of the students' growth over the years rather than focus on their immediate results on this problem.

POW 11 *High-Low Differences*

In this POW, you are to investigate a certain rule for generating a sequence of numbers.

The rule involves the repeated use of a three-step arithmetic process.

The following example shows how this three-step process works if you start with the number 473.

Step 1. Arrange the digits from largest to smallest: 743

Step 2. Arrange the digits from smallest to largest: 347

Step 3. Subtract the smaller number from the larger one.

$$743$$
$$-\ 347$$
$$\overline{396}$$

The result of subtraction, 396, is called the **high-low difference** for the original number 473.

Continued on next page

Tonight's homework is intended to help students get started on POW 11. The POW is scheduled to be discussed on Day 29.

(The name comes from the fact that 743 is the highest number you can get from the digits of the number 473, and 347 is the lowest.)

You can then take 396 and find *its* high-low difference, and then take that number and find *its* high-low difference, and so on. We will call the numbers you get in this manner the **high-low sequence** for the starting number 473.

Your task in this POW is to investigate these sequences for various starting numbers. You should continue with each high-low sequence until something interesting happens.

Begin by investigating three-digit starting numbers (such as 473). Look for patterns in the high-low sequence and for reasons that explain what you see happening.

Then see what happens with four-digit numbers, five-digit numbers, and so forth.

Your assignment has two components.

- Figure out as much as you can about high-low differences and high-low sequences.

- Explain as much of what you discover as you can.

Write-up

This POW is more like an exploration than a problem-solving process. Use the categories below for your write-up.

1. *Subject of Exploration:* Describe the subject that you are investigating. What questions do you want to explore?

2. *Information Gathering:* Based on your notes (which should be included with your write-up), state what happened in the specific cases you examined.

3. *Conclusions, Explanations, and Conjectures:* Describe any general observations you made or conclusions you reached. Wherever possible, explain why your particular conclusions are true. That is, try to *prove* your general statements. But also include *conjectures*, which are statements that you only *think* are true.

4. *Open Questions:* What questions do you have that you were not able to answer? What other investigations would you do if you had more time?

5. *Evaluation*

Homework 24   Different High-Lows

1. Write the *Subject of Exploration* portion of your write-up for *POW 11: High-Low Differences.*

2. Investigate the high-low sequence for six new starting numbers. Pick two 3-digit numbers, two 4-digit numbers, and two 5-digit numbers.

3. Record one observation from your results in Question 2 that might be helpful in working on the POW.

Homework 24: Different High-Lows

Tonight's homework assignment will ensure that students get started on *POW 11: High-Low Differences.*

Situations for Systems

Students solve another problem involving two linear equations.

Mathematical Topics

- Finding algebraic expressions for situations that involve constant rates of consumption
- Solving problems by using graphs

Outline of the Day

In Class

1. Discuss *Homework 24: Different High-Lows*
   - Clear up any uncertainties about the assignment

2. *Water Conservation*
   - Students find algebraic formulas to describe rates of water consumption

3. Discuss *Water Conservation*
   - Focus on using a graph to determine when two families will have the same amount of water remaining

At Home

Homework 25: The Big Buy

1. Discussion of Homework 24: Different High-Lows

"Do you have any questions about what your task is?"

The main purpose of the homework was to ensure that students begin work in earnest on *POW 11: High-Low Differences.* You can ask the class if they have questions about how high-low differences or sequences are defined—that is, questions that are needed to clarify the assignment—but don't get into a discussion of the substance of the exploration, since students should put in serious investigative time on their own.

Water Conservation

Nevada seemed like a desert to the emigrants, who had been following large rivers most of the way from Westport. As you have seen, water was a very precious commodity on the Overland Trail, and travelers had to be careful not to run out.

They kept track of their water use, planning for the next opportunity to refill their water containers.

1. The Stevens family had a 50-gallon water container. In an effort to conserve water, they reduced their daily consumption to three gallons per day.

   If they began with a full container, how many gallons of water would they have left after three days? Eight days? Twelve days? *X* days?

2. The Muster family was larger. They had a 100-gallon water container. Their daily consumption was eight gallons per day.

   If they began with a full container, how many gallons of water would they have left after three days? Eight days? Twelve days? *X* days?

3. Use your answers to the last part of Questions 1 and 2 to graph each family's water supply. Use *number of days* for the horizontal axis and *amount of water left* for the vertical axis. Graph both functions on the same set of axes.

4. Is there a time when both families would have the same amount of water left? If so, when would it happen and how much water would both families have at that time?

5. In how many days would each family run out of water?

2. Water Conservation

This assignment is set in northeast Nevada. Point out on the map where the wagons are on the trail.

The goal of this assignment is to give students more experience both in writing rules for situations and in finding the common solution to a pair of equations.

As students work, you can give various groups pens and overhead transparencies to use in preparing for their class presentations. You can let groups who work more slowly make presentations on Questions 1 through 3, to ensure that they get an opportunity to make presentations, and leave Questions 4 and 5 for faster groups.

3. Discussion of Water Conservation

Most of this activity's content should be familiar to students. If they have difficulty with Question 4, remind them that one of the lines represents the amount of water the Stevens family has on a given day and the other line represents the amount of water the Muster family has on a given day. They should see that if they want to find a day when both families have the same amount of water, then they want to look for a point that is on both lines.

Identify the solutions to Question 5—that is, the points where the graphs cross the *x*-axis—as the **x-intercepts** of the graphs.

Homework 25: The Big Buy
(see next page)

In this assignment, students will use a pair of graphs to compare different rates of pay. The idea of point of intersection plays an important role in this problem.

Homework 25 — The Big Buy

Seve and Jillian Vicaro want to make some money over the spring break from school. They ask their parents to let them work around the house to earn the money. Their parents agree, since Jillian and Seve are saving to buy graphing calculators.

Dad tells Jillian that he will give her a starting bonus of $10, and then pay her $5 an hour for the work she does around the house. Mom offers Seve a slightly different deal. She will give him $40 to start, but only $3 an hour.

1. Write two separate equations, one for Jillian and one for Seve, expressing how much money each has earned (including their starting money) in terms of time worked. (Use x for the number of hours worked and y for the amount earned.)

2. Graph both equations on the same set of axes. (Be sure you know which graph is for which person.)

3. If the graphing calculator costs $72, who will be able to buy one with the least work time? Explain your answer.

4. If the graphing calculator costs $100, who will be able to buy one with the least work time? Explain your answer.

5. For what price must the calculator sell in order for Jillian and Seve to earn that amount with the same number of hours of work? Explain your answer.

Days 26-27

How Fast Should You Go?

This page in the student book introduces Days 26 and 27.

You can probably *walk* faster than the Overland Trail wagons sometimes traveled. Imagine what the settlers would think of today's automobiles and speed limits! Whatever the speed at which a vehicle travels, it has to fit the situation. Not unlike today's travelers, settlers on the trail had to think about the rate at which they traveled in order to compensate for poor weather and to keep up with one another.

Don't lose heart—you're almost to California.

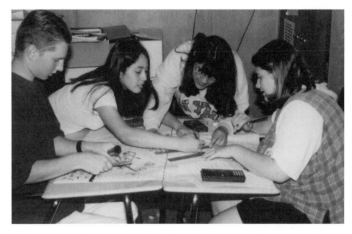

Mark Hansen, Robin LeFevre, Jennifer Rodriguez, and Karla Viaramontes make a group graph.

Working with Rate, Time, and Distance

Students work intuitively with the relationships between rate, time, and distance.

Mathematical Topics

- Working with rate, time, and distance

Outline of the Day

In Class

1. Discuss *Homework 25: The Big Buy*
2. *Catching Up*
   - Students work with rates of travel in problem situations
3. Discuss *Catching Up*
   - Identify the elements of **rate**, **time**, and **distance** within the problem contexts

- Work on developing general formulas from the individual examples

At Home

Homework 26: Water for One More

- Students will need to know the number of people in the Overland Trail family for which they are responsible

Special Materials Needed

- Dice (two per group)

Discuss With Your Colleagues

Introducing Formulas

On Day 26, in discussing *Catching Up,* you may be tempted to give students the general formula $rt = d$ or to push them to make this formalization on their own.

Discuss with your colleagues the different ways in which students worked on *Catching Up,* and compare these approaches with your own algebra education. You can often take a cue from students about when they are ready to put ideas like rate, time, and distance into a general formula and when they are better off working with each problem on its own.

1. Discussion of *Homework 25: The Big Buy*

Ask students to share and to check each other's solutions in their groups. This assignment had them go straight to the equation without specifically suggesting that they look at cases or make an In-Out table. If necessary, remind them that the table is always a good tool to use if they are having difficulty understanding a situation.

You can circulate among the groups as they compare results, to see if any class discussion is needed. You may also want students to graph their equations on their graphing calculators and to check their answers.

2. *Catching Up*
(see facing page)

Catching up involves questions about rates of travel and provides an opportunity for students to explore the basic relationship between rate, time, and distance. The activity also gives students more experience creating a general rule from specific examples of a situation. *Note:* Students will have more problems involving rate, time, and distance in the course of this unit.

The two problems in this activity are not very different from each other, so we suggest that you assign one problem to half the groups and the other problem to the remaining groups.

Group will need dice to begin the activity. Perhaps each group could have a pair of toy covered wagons or some other manipulative to use to act out the scenario.

If groups have trouble getting started on the problems, you might want to give some hints.

For Question 1, you can use the sequence of questions below.

- How far will the main group have traveled by September 12?
  (If necessary, ask how many days the main group will have been traveling by September 12 and how fast they are going.)

- How many days will you have in which to travel that distance?

For Question 2, you can ask these questions.

- How many hours will the main group need to travel to reach Reno?
  (If necessary, ask how fast the main group is traveling and how far they are going.)

- How many hours will you have in which to travel the same distance as the main group?

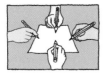

Catching up

1. *By a Specific Date*

Your family has arrived a little late in Winnemucca, Nevada. (Roll one die to find the exact date in September when you arrive there.) You find the following note from your cousin's family:

It is early on the morning of September 1, and we are leaving Winnemucca today with the wagon train. We hope you can catch up with us. We plan to make 15 miles a day. We hope to see you in a few days.

Continued on next page

Then have diamond card students report on how they analyzed and answered the question. Remind groups that when they make their reports, they will first have to describe the problem, for the benefit of groups that did not work on it, before they discuss their solution.

Assume that you will need the rest of today (the day you arrive) and all of tomorrow to get ready, and that you will leave the day after tomorrow.

How fast will you have to travel (in miles per day) to catch up by the end of September 12?

2. *By a Specific Place*

It is 10 A.M. on September 19. Your wagon has just broken a wheel outside of Lovelock, Nevada, and you have to stop to fix it. (Roll two dice and add the numbers to find out how many hours of traveling time you will lose.)

The rest of the wagon train proceeds without you. They are traveling at a rate of 2 miles per hour.

You want to catch up with them by the time they get to Reno, Nevada, which is 80 miles away. Assume that once you get going again, you'll be traveling the same hours as the wagon train.

How fast will you have to travel to catch up by Reno? Give your answer to the nearest tenth of a mile per hour.

3. Discussion of *Catching Up*

"What does '15 miles per day' represent in Question 1?"
"What does '80 miles' represent in Question 2?"
"What are you trying to find in each problem?"

As groups make their presentations, look for opportunities to identify the key elements of **rate**, **time**, and **distance**. Here are a few suggestions.

- In Question 1, get students to identify "15 miles per day" as the main group's *rate* and "12 days" as the main group's *time*, and help them to realize that they use this information to find the *distance* to be covered.

- In Question 2, ask students to identify the information they are given. They should identify "2 miles per hour" as a *rate*, and "80 miles" as a *distance*, and realize that they use this information to find the amount of *time* that the main group is traveling.

- In both problems, once students have figured out what is happening with the main group, they are looking for their own *rate*, using information about *time* and *distance*.

Keep in mind that different groups will get different answers, depending on their dice rolls.

> It is important that students have the opportunity to work with the ideas of rate, time, and distance without having to formalize them in terms of the equation $rt = d$. Working with these ideas may be difficult for many students, and they need time to understand them and to reason problems out on their own.

> *Note:* As suggested at the beginning of Day 26, you may find it helpful to discuss with colleagues whether to give the students formulas such as $rt = d$ or to let them create their own abstractions at their own pace.

• *Generalizing the results*

"Can you develop a formula for the rate required in terms of the numbers on the dice?"

Once they have completed their presentations, you might ask groups to work on developing a formula for the rate required in terms of the numbers on the dice. As in many earlier problems, one of the best approaches is to have students put into words the process they used for a specific case.

> *Note:* Having students create such a general formula will be good preparation for tonight's homework, in which students will be asked to develop a similar formula.

Homework 26: *Water for One More*
(see next page)

Tonight's homework requires students to have their Overland Trail family information available.

Homework 26   Water for One More

It is September 23, and you are stopping for the night in what is now Reno, Nevada. (The town got that name in 1868.)

While you are stopped, a straggler comes by who fell off his horse and got left behind by his wagon train. You have decided to let him ride with you for a while and to share your supplies with him.

With an extra person, you need to ration your water more carefully. You expect to reach a river by the end of the day on September 29, where you can replenish your water, and where he will probably be able to rejoin his group. Had the straggler not joined you, you would have had three gallons per day for each person.

1. Give the size of the Overland Trail family for which you are responsible.

2. Based on that family size, how much water can you now allow per day for each person (that is, with the addition of one more person)?

3. Suppose instead that your Overland Trail family contained ten people (with three gallons per day for each person). How much water would you have per person with the straggler included?

4. Answer Question 3 for the case where the Overland Trail family contains 20 people.

5. Generalize Question 3 to the case where the Overland Trail family contains x people.

The mathematics in the homework is similar to that of the classwork, but uses rate of water consumption rather than rate of travel, and asks students explicitly to generalize their results.

Although the scenario of this problem is similar to *Homework 21: Biddy Mason,* the variable here is the size of the Overland Trail family rather than the size of the group that is joining.

Compatible Rates

Students continue to work with rate, time, and distance.

Mathematical Topics

- Working with various types of rates
- Interpreting word problems

Outline of the Day

In Class

1. Discuss *Homework 26: Water for One More*
   - Compare the use of *rate* in different contexts, such as rate of consumption and rate of travel

2. *Catching Up by Saturday Night*
   - Students find pairs of rates to fit a given situation

3. Discuss *Catching Up by Saturday Night*
   - Encourage students to represent the problem with graphs, tables, and equations

At Home

Homework 27: *Catching Up in Auburn*

1. Discussion of *Homework 26: Water for One More*

You can let two or three volunteers tell the class what happened with their Overland Trail families. Some students may use the time duration of the journey in their calculation, even though it doesn't affect the final result.

For example, with a family size of 12, they might figure out that the total amount of water initially was $6 \cdot 12 \cdot 3 = 216$ gallons (6 days times 12 people times 3 gallons per person per day).

They would then figure that with an additional person there would be $216 \div 13 \approx 16.6$ gallons per person, which comes to $16.6 \div 6 \approx 2.8$ gallons per person per day when the straggler is included.

This approach gives the same answer as figuring $12 \cdot 3 = 36$ gallons per day, since that comes to $36 \div 13 \approx 2.8$ gallons per person per day with the straggler included.

"How would the result change if the time given for the journey to the river had been different?"

If these approaches don't both come up, you might ask how the result would change if the time given for the journey to the river had been different. Students should realize that it doesn't matter, and that in the first approach, they are both multiplying and dividing by 6.

"How does the result vary from family to family?"
"Is there a bigger impact on big families or on small families?"

Discuss how the result varied from family to family, and why. In particular, you might ask,

Is there a bigger impact on big families or on small families?

Students should realize that adding one more person makes a bigger impact on a small family, and this should seem reasonable to them.

The general formula that students get in Question 5 will probably depend on the method they used. With the first method, they are likely to get something like $\frac{18x}{x+1} \div 6$, while with the second method, they might get $\frac{3x}{x+1}$.

You may want to have students graph the functions defined by their general expressions.

Note: If students get different expressions, you can mention that they will look at the issue of two expressions having the same meaning in the Year 2 unit *Solve It!*

• *Real-life considerations*

There are many real-life considerations that could lead to variations in the homework problem. You may want to take time to discuss some of them. Here are a few examples.

• What if you want to keep a reserve water supply?

• What if the stranger gets only a subsistence allotment—for example, half of what everyone else gets?

• What if you take into account the fact that some of the water is needed for general purposes, rather than allotted only a per-person basis?

• *Different kinds of rate problems*

Bring out that both the homework problem and the two problems in yesterday's activity, *Catching Up,* can be thought of as rate problems. The problems in *Catching Up* involved rate of travel, while the homework problem involved rate of consumption.

> The appropriate formula for rate of travel is
>
> $$\text{rate of travel} \cdot \text{time} = \text{distance}$$
>
> while the appropriate formula for water consumption is
>
> $$\text{rate of consumption} \cdot \text{number of people} = \text{quantity consumed}$$

In both cases, the problem was to find a rate that led to compatible totals—either miles traveled or water consumed. This analogy need not be pushed too far, but some effort should be made to highlight the similarity between the two problems.

2. *Catching Up by Saturday Night*

(see next page)

In yesterday's *Catching Up* problems, the travel rate of the rest of the wagon train was given. Therefore, once the student knew how much time had been lost, there was a unique answer for the rate at which the group left behind had to travel in order to catch up.

In today's activity, *Catching Up by Saturday Night,* and in the related problem in tonight's *Homework 27: Catching Up in Auburn,* this is changed. These problems eliminate the uncertainty about the amount of time lost, and focus instead on the two rates—the rate of the wagon train as a whole, and the rate of the group left behind. The question is presented in a way that might be interpreted algebraically as one equation with two unknowns. In other words, the students are looking for *a pair of rates* that satisfy a given set of conditions.

Have students work on the activity in their groups, and then bring the class together for a discussion.

If the problem seems too open-ended, you might suggest to each group that they pick a specific rate for the main wagon train—for example, by rolling four dice—and then figure out the necessary rate for the travelers that have to catch up.

Catching Up by Saturday Night

It is Wednesday morning, October 1, and you are in the mountains the settlers call the Sierra Nevada. Your daughter has given birth during the night to a healthy baby girl.

You decide your wagon should stop for a day to allow her to rest briefly. You will start moving again Thursday morning, but the rest of the wagon train is going to continue traveling this morning.

You want to be able to catch up with the rest of the wagon train by the end of Saturday, so that you will be able to celebrate the birth of your new granddaughter with your fellow travelers that night.

You confer with the wagon train leader Wednesday morning before the wagon train leaves. Together, you want to agree on the rates at which you and the wagon train will each travel so that you can catch up with them late Saturday. (The wagon train will travel the same amount of time each day and you will travel the same amount of time each day, although your rate will differ from the wagon train's. The leader is willing to let you propose the two rates.)

1. Figure out a possible pair of rates—one for the main part of the wagon train and one for you—so that you will catch up with the main group at the end of Saturday. Express your rates in *miles per day*.

2. Using these rates, figure out how far down the trail you and the wagon train will be when you catch up to them.

3. Find three more pairs of rates that satisfy Question 1, and then answer Question 2 for each of them.

3. Discussion of *Catching Up by Saturday Night*

Let various groups share their results and discuss how they got them.

Different groups will probably come up with different pairs of rates for this problem, and there may be differences in method of solution. One likely method is to pick a rate for the main group (say, 15 miles per day), compute the distance they travel (60 miles in four days), and then figure out the rate needed by the small group to cover the same distance in three days (20 miles per day).

The different combinations of rates can be arranged in an In-Out table. (There is no particular basis here for deciding which rate should be the *In* and which the *Out*; either choice makes sense.)

"What do you expect the graph to look like?"

Help the class to see the In-Out table as information for both a graph and an equation. Perhaps before plotting the points, you might want to ask the students what they expect the graph to look like.

Some students may be able to see at once that the small group's rate needs to be $\frac{4}{3}$ times that of the main group, because they are traveling three days instead of four. This relationship might be developed out of the In-Out table if nobody comes up with it directly.

The fact that the ordered pairs form a straight line may also be a clue to the relationship. One way or another, students should develop an equation like $R_2 = \frac{4}{3} R_1$ (where R_2 is the rate of the individual wagon and R_1 is the rate of the main group). If this relationship is discovered from the table or the graph, ask the class to think about an explanation for this phenomenon. (You don't need to force this if they don't see it.)

Homework 27: Catching Up in Auburn

(see next page)

Tonight's homework assignment is a variation on the problem in *Catching Up by Saturday Night*.

If students don't have dice at home, you may want to have them do the dice rolling for Question 1 in class.

Homework 27   Catching Up at Auburn

You are now northwest of Reno, Nevada. You are intrigued by the man who runs an inn and trading post, and you decide to spend two days visiting.

The innkeeper is James P. Beckwourth.

About James Beckwourth

James Beckwourth, born around 1798 in Virginia, was the son of an African American woman and her master, a white man. At 19, during a fight with one of his bosses, he

Continued on next page

slugged his way to freedom and subsequently traveled from one end of the continent to the other.

On the trail, he fought with and against several Native American nations, and also served as a scout for the United States Army in the war against the Seminole. A contemporary of Kit Carson and Davy Crockett, Beckwourth was part of the brutal frontier tradition. He was said to have "fought and killed with ease and pleasure."

He also married often. After marrying a Crow woman, he was adopted into the Crow Nation and led the Crow in battle.

In 1850, Beckwourth located a pass through the Sierra Nevada into the American Valley that became a gateway to California during the gold rush. The mountain peak, the town, and the pass still bear his name. For a number of years, a Denver street and church also carried his name.

Your Problem

Since you are going to spend time with Beckwourth, you will need to make arrangements with the rest of the wagon train. You want to catch up with them as they reach Auburn, California, which is 140 miles away.

You confer with the wagon train leader, to arrange to meet at the river. The leader tells you the rate at which the wagon train will move. You then have to find a compatible rate so that you and the wagon train will arrive in Auburn at the same time.

1. Roll a die four times and use the sum as the wagon train's rate (in *miles per day*). Based on this rate, find the rate at which you will have to travel in order to catch up at Auburn.

2. Do Question 1 twice more, with different wagon train rates. (The leader is unpredictable.)

3. Make an In-Out table that shows the relationship between the wagon train's rate and your rate.

4. Graph the relationship in Question 3.

5. For each of your results in Questions 1 and 2, figure out how many days you will have to travel after you leave Beckwourth.

6. Suppose the wagon train travels x miles per day.

   a. Describe how to figure out what your rate should be.

   b. Find an algebraic expression for this rate in terms of x.

California at Last!

You've finally arrived in California. As you'll see, life in this state wasn't all golden. You'll also see how the mathematics of expenses and profits played a role in people's everyday decisions.

Perhaps the portfolio for this unit ought to be called a scrapbook. Did you bring your camera along on your trip?

This page in the student book introduces Days 28 and 29.

Ken Weaver writes the cover letter for his portfolio.

DAY 28 *The California Experience*

The Overland Trail travelers arrive in California and begin to look for gold.

Mathematical Topics

- Continued work with rates
- Profit and loss

Outline of the Day

In Class

1. Select presenters for tomorrow's discussion of *POW 11: High-Low Differences*

2. Discuss *Homework 27: Catching Up in Auburn*

3. Have students read *The California Experience* for historical background to the culmination of the unit

4. *Getting the Gold*
   - Students find the profit a family might make using two different methods for getting gold

5. Discuss *Getting the Gold*
   - (Optional) After presentations, have students develop general formulas

At Home

Homework 28: California Reflections

1. POW Presentation Preparation

Presentations of *POW 11: High-Low Differences* are scheduled for tomorrow. Choose three students to make POW presentations, and give them pens and overhead transparencies to take home to use in their preparations.

2. Discussion of Homework 27: Catching Up in Auburn

"How did you obtain the rate for the individual wagon from the rate for the main group?"

"Is the relationship linear?"

You can begin by asking each club card student to give one of the rate combinations that they found and to explain how they obtained the rate for the individual wagon from the rate for the main group. (The explanations will probably include their results for Question 5.) If the explanations become repetitive, you need not have them explain their work for every combination.

As the combinations are given, you can put them in a collective In-Out table, and plot the corresponding points. Students should see that the relationship between the rates is not linear.

If no one found a general expression, you can either leave it an open problem or suggest that they look at the process in steps, tracing their work in the individual cases.

For example, they might go through the following steps.

- How long did it take for the main group to get to Auburn (in days)?

- How many days will the individual wagon have for its travel to Auburn?

- At what rate will the individual wagon have to move in order to get to Auburn in that amount of time?

It is virtually impossible to get an equation for this function by inspecting the In-Out table. Students must get their rule by thinking how they would calculate their speed if they knew the speed of the main wagon. The relationship can be expressed by the equation below (or something equivalent).

$$y = \frac{140}{\frac{140}{x} - 2}$$

If the class does find the general equation, you can have them graph the function on their calculators. There are some interesting areas to explore, since this equation is only meaningful for the problem for certain values of x. Use your judgment about how much exploration to do.

The California Experience

Who were the people in California in the 1850s?

Of course, Native Americans were there, probably for millennia. Some 300 different nations, including the Modoc, Washo, Maidu, Pomo, Cahuilla, and Miwok, held territory, in what is now known as California.

Continued on next page

3. Background Reading: *The California Experience*

Sound the trumpets, bang the gong, have the class give itself three cheers because they have made it to California.

Then came the Spanish. Out of their conquest and mixture with the Native Americans came a new culture and a new nation called Mexico, which became politically independent of Spain in 1821.

Indeed, that new Mexican nation claimed all of what is now the state of California, as well as all of Nevada and Utah and parts of Arizona, New Mexico, Colorado, and Wyoming. But in 1846, the United States provoked a war with Mexico in an attempt to gain territory. The United States won the war, which ended in 1848 with the Treaty of Guadalupe Hidalgo. In this treaty, Mexico was forced to cede much of what is now the southwestern United States.

Although the first wagon trains left Missouri for California in 1841, the great migration of the mid-nineteenth century was spurred by the discovery of gold in 1848, just nine days before the signing of the Treaty of Guadalupe Hidalgo.

The arrival of hundreds of thousands, many in search of gold, permanently changed the lives of the people who had been there before and led to the destruction of whole nations of native peoples.

The gold rush also led to thousands of people being brought from China to work as menial laborers. Though in 1850 there were only a few hundred Chinese in California, by 1852 about 10 percent of the population was Chinese, many of whom lived in slave-like conditions.

Those who traveled on the California Trail in search of gold often ended up destitute, and a number of women resorted to prostitution to survive.

So the California experience was a mixture of many things. Just a very few became rich from the mining of gold.

But then have students read *The California Experience*, which shows that the great migration of the mid-nineteenth century was not a positive experience for all who undertook it.

Tonight's homework asks students to reflect on the history of the period.

Getting the Gold

Many of those who made the long trek to California were in search of gold. Though few were able to get rich, many tried.

One of the most common ways to get gold was to pan for it in streams.

To pan for gold, all a person needed was a $9 shovel, a $50 burro, and a $1 pan. A person could get an ounce of gold each day, on the average, by panning.

One ingenious person discovered a way to get gold from a stream by using a trough. The trough was a long chute that miners set in the stream and rocked back and forth to separate the gold from the silt of the stream.

Although it was more expensive to get started with the trough method, that technique produced about twice as much gold each day as the pan method. To use a trough, a person needed a team of two burros, a shovel, and a trough. The trough cost $311.

At that time, gold was worth $15 an ounce. The following questions involve the amount of profit (income minus expenses) from each method after a certain number of days. (A loss of money is considered a negative profit.)

1. How much profit will each method yield after 16 days?

2. How much profit will each method yield after 30 days?

3. How much profit will each method yield after 5 days?

4. Make two graphs on the same set of axes: one graph should show the profit from panning; the other should show the profit from using a trough. (The horizontal axis is the number of days.)

5. How many days will it take for a miner using each method to break even?

6. After how many days will the two methods yield the same amount of money?

4. *Getting the Gold*

After students read *The California Experience* to put the gold rush in perspective, have them work in groups on *Getting the Gold*. Earlier problems asked students to determine rates of travel and rates of consumption. Now students will look at rates of profit.

You can ask groups that finish early to try to develop algebraic expressions for the amount of profit after *x* days.

5. Discussion of *Getting the Gold*

Have a group or two present their methods of working out the results. By now, most students should be fairly comfortable with the ideas involved in this problem.

If any group developed a formula for the profit after x days, you can ask them to make a presentation. If not, you can ask students to work on that question as time allows.

Homework 28: *California Reflections*

(see facing page)

Tonight's homework asks students to think about the broader social issues during the time of the California gold rush.

Homework 28   California Reflections

The California Experience outlines some of the historical and social background of the period of the gold rush.

Write about your own feelings concerning this period of American history.

You may want to talk about the group or groups you identify with, about issues of justice or injustice, or about the process of social change.

You may also want to comment on how your ideas about the period have changed over the course of this unit.

POW 11
Presentations

Students present POW 11.

Mathematical Topics

- Exploring numerical situations
- Explaining numerical discoveries

Outline of the Day

In Class
1. Discuss *Homework 28: California Reflections*
2. Presentations of *POW 11: High-Low Differences*

At Home
Homework 29: Beginning Portfolio Selection

1. Discussion of *Homework 28: California Reflections*

You can let students share ideas in their groups or as a whole class.

2. Presentations of *POW 11: High-Low Differences*

"Did you have any observations that weren't mentioned in the presentations?"

Have three students make their POW presentations. Unlike many POWs, this one has no solutions—just observations. Allow other students to add any ideas they have that are not mentioned by the presenters.

For the case of three-digit numbers with distinct digits, you might expect to hear some of these observations.

- Every high-low difference has the number 9 in the middle.

- After a few rounds, you eventually get the difference of 495.

- The digits of every high-low difference add up to 18.

- Every high-low difference is a multiple of 99.

Students may not notice all of these things, or they may state them in different ways. It isn't important for them to know these facts, but rather for them to learn something about the process of exploring a problem.

You can also ask students to explain any phenomena they observed.

Here are some further questions that can be explored.

- What happens if the starting number has repeat digits, such as 585?

- What happens if the starting number has a zero, such as 703?

Though the example in the POW itself uses three-digit numbers, students should have explored numbers of other lengths, at least in *Homework 24: Different High-Lows*. If students don't mention numbers of other lengths, ask explicitly what they found out about such other cases.

Homework 29: Beginning Portfolio Selection
(see facing page)

Tonight students will begin the first stage of putting together their unit portfolios. Remind them to bring all of their work from the unit to class tomorrow so they can complete their portfolio work.

Homework 29

Beginning Portfolio Selection

The meaning and use of graphs played an important role in this unit.

Select one assignment from the unit that illustrates how graphs can describe a problem situation.

Select another assignment that illustrates how graphs can be used to make a decision about a problem situation.

Explain how each of these assignments helped you to understand the meaning and use of graphs.

(Making these selections and explaining them are the first steps toward compiling your portfolio for this unit.)

DAY 30 *Portfolios*

Mathematical Topics

• Reviewing the unit and preparing portfolios

Outline of the Day

In Class

1. Remind students that they will take unit assessments tomorrow and tomorrow night

2. *"The Overland Trail" Portfolio*
   • Students write cover letters and assemble portfolios for the unit

At Home

Students complete portfolios and prepare for assessments

---

1. Reminder: Unit Assessments Tomorrow

Remind students that they will get their in-class and take-home unit assessments tomorrow.

2. *"The Overland Trail" Portfolio*

(see next page)

Tell students to read over the instructions in *"The Overland Trail" Portfolio* carefully. Then they are to look over all of their work from the unit.

They will have done part of the selection process in last night's homework, and their main task today is to write their cover letters.

If students do not complete the task, you may want them to take the materials home and to finish compiling their portfolios for homework. Be

---

"The Overland Trail" Portfolio

Now that *The Overland Trail* is completed, it is time to put together your portfolio for the unit. Compiling this portfolio has three parts.

- Writing a cover letter that summarizes the unit

- Choosing papers to include from your work in the unit

- Writing about your reactions to using a graphing calculator

Cover Letter for "The Overland Trail"

Look back over *The Overland Trail* and describe the main mathematical ideas of the unit. This description should give an overview of how the key ideas were developed.

As part of the compilation of your portfolio, you will select activities that you think were important in developing the key ideas of this unit. In your cover letter, you should include an explanation of why you selected the particular items you did.

Selecting Papers from "The Overland Trail"

Your portfolio for *The Overland Trail* should contain the items on this list.

- *Homework 29: Beginning Portfolio Selection*

  Include the two activities about graphs that you selected in *Homework 29: Beginning Portfolio* Selection, along with the explanation you wrote about how these assignments helped you to understand the meaning and use of graphs.

- *Homework 28: California Reflections*

  This assignment should be included in order to reflect the historical elements of the unit and your reaction to them.

- *Homework 13: Situations, Graphs, Tables, and Rules*

  This assignment is included because it summarizes the connections between situations, graphs, tables, and rules—four different ways of representing functions.

Continued on next page

sure that they bring the portfolio back tomorrow with the cover letter as its first item. They should also bring any other work that they think will be of help on tomorrow's unit assessments. The remainder of their work can be kept at home.

- An activity about the use of variables

  Select an item from the unit that illustrates or helped you to understand the meaning or use of variables, and explain your selection.

- An activity about rates

  The unit included problems about rates in several different contexts. Select an activity that illustrates important points about rates or that helped you to understand how to work with rates. Explain your selection.

- A Problem of the Week

  Select one of the four POWs you completed during this unit (*The Haybaler Problem, Around the Horn, On Your Own,* or *High-Low Differences*).

- Other quality work

  Select one or two other pieces of work that represent your best efforts. (These can be any work from the unit—Problem of the Week, homework, classwork, presentation, and so forth.)

Graphing With and Without Calculators

Many of the problems in this unit involved graphs, and you learned how to use a graphing calculator to make graphs. Write about your reactions to using this tool. You may want to address the questions below.

- What are the advantages of using the calculator to make graphs?
- What are the advantages of doing graphs by hand?
- How does each approach help in your understanding of graphs and in your ability to use them to solve problems?

Homework: Prepare for Assessments

Students' homework for tonight is to prepare for tomorrow's assessments by reviewing the mathematical ideas of the unit.

Students do the in-class assessment and can begin the take-home assessment.

Special Materials Needed

- *In-Class Assessment for "The Overland Trail"*
- *Take-Home Assessment for "The Overland Trail"*

Outline of the Day

In Class

1. Introduce assessments
   - Students do *In-Class Assessment for "The Overland Trail"*
   - Students begin *Take-Home Assessment for "The Overland Trail"*

At Home

Students complete *Take-Home Assessment for "The Overland Trail"*

---

1. End-of-Unit Assessments

Note: The in-class portion of unit assessments are intentionally short so that time pressure will not be a factor in students' ability to do well. The IMP *Teaching Handbook* contains general information about the purpose of end-of-unit assessments and how to use them.

Tell students that today they will get two tests—one that they will finish in class and one that they can start in class and will be able to finish at home. The take-home part should be handed in tomorrow.

Tell students that they are allowed to use graphing calculators, notes from previous work, and so forth, in their work on the assessment. (They have to do without the graphing calculators on the take-home portion.)

The assessments are provided in Appendix B for you to duplicate.

In-Class Assessment for "The Overland Trail"

The questions in this assessment are about a modern-day move from Kansas City, Missouri, to San Francisco, California.

Unlike the settlers of 1850, your family will travel on superhighways with a large rental truck and a van. The distance between the two cities is 1500 miles.

In answering the questions, be sure to show your reasoning, not just give an answer. Assume that your average speed is 50 miles per hour.

1. Suppose you estimate that you can drive for an average of six hours on a typical day of the trip. How many days will the trip last at this rate?

2. Construct an In-Out table in which the *In* column contains the number of hours of driving per day and the *Out* column shows how many days the trip will last.

3. Plot the points from your table in Question 2, to show the number of days in the trip as a function of how many hours you are willing to drive per day.

4. Create an algebraic expression that shows how to compute the number of days required for a trip like this (not necessarily 1500 miles—you should represent the distance by a variable). This expression should not contain any numbers and you should clearly define the symbols in it.

Take-Home Assessment for *The Overland Trail*

As in the *In-Class Assessment for "The Overland Trail,"* the questions below have to do with a modern-day move.

Your family is traveling on superhighways with a large rental truck and a van.

1. *Fuel Economies*

Each time one of the vehicles stops for gas, you make a note of how much gas the vehicle has used and how many miles it has traveled.

a. Using the data in the tables below, draw two graphs *on the same set of axes*, comparing total miles traveled to total gallons of gas used for each vehicle:

Van		Truck	
Total amount of gas used so far	Total number of miles traveled so far	Total amount of gas used so far	Total number of miles traveled so far
18	400	36	300
28	700	65	600
42	990	100	850
52	1250	138	1100

b. Reading from the graph, estimate how many gallons of gas the truck had guzzled by the time you traveled 800 miles. And how about the van?

c. Estimate how many miles each vehicle can travel on a gallon of gas.

Continued on next page

Homework: Complete *Take-Home Assessment for "The Overland Trail"*

Students should bring the completed assessment to class tomorrow. As with all work done at home, students may collaborate or get assistance, but they should report this fact in their write-up of the assessment.

2. *Van Repairs*

One morning, as you attempt to get started, you find that the van won't start. The garage mechanic says that the fuel pump needs replacement and that the work can be done fairly quickly, in about two hours.

The family decides that Mom and you should head out in the truck towards that night's stop, 400 miles down the highway. Dad and the rest of the family will remain behind and either catch up with you during the day or meet you tonight at the motel where you have reservations.

a. Suppose that the truck travels at 45 miles per hour, that the van goes at 55 miles per hour (once it is fixed), and that the repair actually takes two hours. For the sake of simplicity, assume that neither vehicle makes any stops along the way.

   i. Which vehicle will get to the motel first?

   ii. How far from the motel will the other vehicle be when the first vehicle reaches the motel?

b. Of course, the repair might not take the full two hours, or it might take longer. So now consider the case where the repair actually takes four hours. (In this case, the truck definitely arrives first.)

   How far from the motel will the van be when the truck reaches the motel?

c. Now generalize from parts a and b. Suppose that h represents the number of hours of delay for the van. (Assume that h is a number large enough to allow the truck to arrive first.)

   Develop a formula or equation in terms of h that says how far the van will be from the motel when the truck arrives at the motel.

Summing Up

Mathematical Topics

• Summarizing the unit

Outline of the Day

1. Discuss unit assessments
2. Sum up the unit

Note: The commentary that follows is written as if the discussion of unit assessments takes place on the day following the assessments, but you may prefer to delay such a discussion until after you have looked over students' work on the assessments.

1. Discussion of Unit Assessments

You can let students volunteer to explain their work on each of the problems. Encourage questions and alternative explanations from other students.

• In-Class Assessment

You can let volunteers present their ideas about different parts of the assessment.

Questions 1 through 3 are fairly straightforward. In connection with Question 3, students may raise the issue of whether or not the number of days must be an integer.

Question 4 leaves room for a variety of responses. Students may express the number of days required in terms of the total distance, the average speed, and the number of driving hours per day, or they may introduce other factors or may combine factors (for example, combine driving hours with speed to get miles covered per day).

Be sure that variables are clearly defined.

• *Take-Home Assessment*

You can let volunteers share their work on the take-home questions as well.

Question 1 offers another opportunity to talk about average rates and about using graphs to make estimations.

On part i of Question 2a, students should be able to reason through the basic relationship between rate, time, and distance to see that the truck takes $400 \div 45 \approx 8.89$ hours to travel the 400-mile distance, while the van takes $400 \div 55 \approx 7.27$ hours. Since the van starts out two hours later than the truck, the truck arrives first.

There are several ways to work out the answer to part ii of Question 2a. One approach is to point out that the van will still be about 0.38 hours from the motel when the truck arrives, and that this amount of time represents about 21 miles. You can have different students present alternative analyses if they found the answer another way.

Students should reason similarly on Question 2b.

On Question 2c, the most likely approach is for students to follow the reasoning they used in Questions 2a and 2b, replacing "four hours" by "b hours." Using the reasoning described above, they might give their answer as $55(b - 1.62)$.

2. Unit Summary

Let students share their portfolio cover letters as a way to start a discussion to summarize the unit.

"What have you learned in this unit?"

Then let them brainstorm to come up with statements about what they have learned in this unit. This is a good opportunity to review terminology and to place the unit in a broader mathematics context. You may want to emphasize the fact that students combined traditional and nontraditional work in this unit.

Here are some examples of traditional work that was done in the unit.

- Working with variables and algebraic expressions

- Graphing equations and functions

- Expressing problem situations in terms of equations

- Solving problems involving rate, time, and distance

Here are some examples of nontraditional work that was done.

- Working with data and approximating data with linear functions

- Making predictions based on graphical and tabular information

- Using graphing calculators

- Examining how mathematics might have been used in the everyday lives of people in a historical setting.

- Writing about mathematical ideas

Appendix A — Supplemental Problems

This appendix contains a variety of activities that you can use to supplement the regular unit material. These activities are placed at the end of the student materials and fall roughly into two categories.

- Reinforcements, which increase students' understanding and comfort with concepts, techniques, and methods that are discussed in class and that are central to the unit

- Extensions, which allow students to explore ideas beyond the basic unit; some extensions are generalizations or abstractions of ideas offered in the main unit

The supplemental activities are given here and in the student materials in the approximate sequence in which they might be used in the unit. The comments regarding each activity give specific recommendations about how each activity might work within the unit.

In addition to the problems given here, you may want to use supplemental problems from earlier units that were not assigned or completed. The problems listed below may be particularly appropriate.

From *Patterns:*

- *Whose Dog Is That?*
- *A Fractional Life*
- *Infinite Proof*

From *The Game of Pig:*

- *Average Problems*

For more ideas about the use of supplemental activities in the IMP curriculum, see the IMP *Teaching Handbook*.

- *Pick Any Answer* (reinforcement)

  This problem brings out the importance of the sequence in which arithmetic operations are done and gives students experience working with a variable to represent an unknown number. You can assign it after the Day 7 discussion of *Homework 6: Shoelaces*.

- *From Numbers to Algebra and Back Again* (reinforcement)

  This activity is intended primarily as a vehicle for talking about substitution. Students should see that they need only replace the variable by a number to use the formula. You can use this activity as a follow-up to the work on substitution on Day 7, although you might want to use it after *Homework 8: To Kearny by Equation.*

- *Painting the General Cube* (extension)

  This activity is a generalization of the problem in the take-home assessment for *Patterns,* but it can be used even if you did not use that assessment. You can assign it at any point in the unit.

- *More Bales of Hay* (extension)

  Experimentation with numbers is the essence of this problem, which is a follow-up to *POW 8: The Haybaler Problem.* It is probably best to wait until after the discussion of the POW before assigning this problem.

- *Classroom Expressions* and *Variables of Your Own* (reinforcements)

  Classroom Expressions and *Variables of Your Own* are two activities you can use to continue the work on the meaningful use of variables. *Classroom Expressions* also introduces the notation of subscripts. (These were optional on Day 7.) You can use these two activities any time after Day 10.

- *Integers Only* (extension)

  Homework 10: If I Could See This Thing involves a function whose outputs should only be integers. This activity introduces students to the *greatest integer* function. You can use it any time after the homework assignment.

- *Movin' West* (extension)

  In addition to developing a general algebraic formula for a rate-of-change situation, students who work on this problem must think about comparative rates of change and do some commonsense reasoning to decide how well the model suggested by their formula might work in the future. This problem might be a suitable thematic follow-up to *Homework 15: Broken Promises.*

- *Spilling the Beans* (reinforcement or extension)

  An essential part of this problem is the need to clearly understand any assumptions one makes. The problem also involves proportional reasoning, which plays an important role in the last unit of Year 1, *Shadows.* You can use this problem at any point in the unit.

- *The Perils of Pauline* (extension)

  There are many ways to set up and solve this problem, which uses the basic rate-time-distance relationship. It fits in well after *Catching Up* on Day 26.

- *High-Low Proofs* (extension)

  Students may have made several observations in *POW 11: High-Low Differences* that they did not prove. This activity offers them an opportunity to look further at that problem. (You may want to save this activity to use as a supplemental problem during the next unit, since the presentations for *POW 11: High-Low Differences* occur so late in *The Overland Trail.*)

The Overland Trail

Appendix

Supplemental Problems

Some of the supplemental problems for *The Overland Trail* extend POWs from this unit. Others continue your work with variables or build on the theme of the western migration. These are some examples.

This page in the student book introduces the supplemental problems.

- *More Bales of Hay* and *High-Low Proofs* pose some questions related to *POW 8: The Haybaler Problem* and *POW 11: High-Low Differences.*

- *Classroom Expressions* and *Variables of Your Own* ask you to form meaningful expressions with variables.

- *Movin' West* and *The Perils of Pauline* pose problems that relate to the movement of people and goods across the country.

Pick Any Answer

Lai Yee has a new trick. He tells someone:

- Pick any number.
- Multiply by 2.
- Now add 8.
- Divide by 2.
- Subtract the number you started with.
- Your answer is 4.

1. Try out Lai Yee's trick. Is the answer always 4? If you think it always is, explain why. If not, explain why it sometimes will be something else.

2. Make up a trick whose answer will always be 5.

3. Pretend that someone gives you a number that he or she wants to be the answer. Using the variable A to stand for that number, make up a trick whose answer will always be A.

From Numbers to Algebra and Back Again

1. *One-and-One Generalization*

In *The Game of Pig*, you found the expected value in the one-and-one situation for a player who gets 60 percent of all shots.

You may have done similar problems using different percentages.

Continued on next page

Interactive Mathematics Program   291

Now consider the general case. Suppose the variable p represents the probability that a player succeeds with a given shot, and assume that this value is the same for every shot.

a. Explain, using the example of $p = 60\%$ as a model, why the expected value for this player is $2p^2 + p(1 - p)$.

b. Use the formula from Question 1a to find the player's expected value for the case in which $p = .9$.

c. What value of p would give an expected value of 1.5 points per one-and-one situation?

2. *Lots of Diagonals*

A quadrilateral has two diagonals. The diagram at the right shows a five-sided polygon with five diagonals.

It turns out (as you may already know) that a polygon with N sides has

$$\frac{N(N-3)}{2}$$

diagonals.

a. Based on this formula, how many diagonals does a 50-sided polygon have?

b. How many sides would a polygon need to have in order to have at least 1000 diagonals?

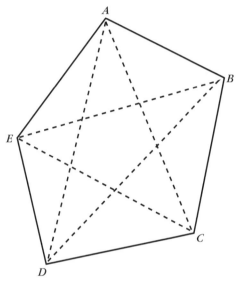

Painting the General Cube

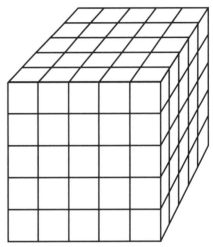

Here is a problem you may have already worked on.

> A cube is 5 inches long in each direction, and is made up of smaller cubes, each of which is 1 inch on every side.
>
> Someone comes along and paints the large cube on all of its faces, including the bottom. None of the paint leaks to the inside.
>
> How many of the smaller cubes have just one face painted? How many have two faces painted? Answer the same question for three, four, five, and six faces.

Now answer the same questions for the situation where the large cube is N inches long on each side (still consisting of smaller cubes, each of which is 1 inch on every side).

More Bales of Hay

In *POW 8: The Haybaler Problem*, you were told that there were five bales of hay, which had been weighed two at a time in all possible combinations. You were given the weights for each of the ten possible pairs of bales and asked to find the weights of the five bales.

That problem had a unique solution.

You might wonder whether there would have been a unique solution, or any solution at all, if the ten weights given for the pairs had been different. That is, are there ten numbers that could not possibly stand for the weights of five bales of hay weighed two at a time in the different combinations?

Note: You may know that a typical bale of hay weighs about 100 pounds. In this problem, however, we want you to focus on the mathematical issues rather than on facts about hay. Therefore, you should think of "bales of hay"

Continued on next page

294

in the problem as representing arbitrary objects, whose weight could be much less or much more than that of a real bale of hay.

1. Before tackling the problem just described, consider the problem below, which involves only three bales of hay.

   > Three bales of hay were weighed two at a time in all three possible combinations. One combination weighed 12 pounds, one combination weighed 15 pounds, and one combination weighed 23 pounds.

   > What were the weights of the three different bales?

   Does this problem have a solution? If so, is the solution unique? Explain your results and how you got them.

2. Now suppose that instead of 12 pounds, 15 pounds, and 23 pounds, the weights given in Question 1 for the three different pairs had been different.

   a. Are there any sets of weights for the three pairs which would have made it impossible to solve Question 1? If so, for which sets of numbers is there a solution and for which sets is there no solution? Explain your answer.

   b. Which sets of weights for the three different pairs give *whole number* solutions for the weights of the individual bales?

3. Now think about a five-bale problem, where there are ten combinations in which to weigh the bales in pairs. Could there be ten numbers that could not be the weights for the ten different pairs of the five bales? Justify your answer.

Classroom Expressions

Variables and summary phrases are useful in many situations other than those involving wagon trains.

In this activity, you will work with a set of variables that relate to a classroom setting.

Subscripts and Superscripts

Mathematicians often use **subscripts** so that they can use similar symbols to represent related quantities. You can think of a subscripted symbol as a two-letter variable for a single quantity.

For example, the combined symbols P_B and P_G are used in this activity to represent the number of pencils that each boy in the classroom has and the number of pencils that each girl in the classroom has.

The subscript, such as B, is written below and to the right of the main symbol, P. The combined symbol P_B is usually read *P sub B*.

You need to exercise care in writing subscripted variables so that they don't look like the product of two separate variables.

Note: A symbol written *above* and to the right of the main symbol, the way we write exponents, is called a **superscript.**

Continued on next page

Variables for the Classroom

The list of variables for the classroom setting is shown below. As in *Ox Expressions,* you should assume that the values of the variables are constant in all cases. For example, assume that every boy has the same number of pencils.

Symbol   **Meaning**

B the number of **B**oys in the classroom

G the number of **G**irls in the classroom

P_B the number of **P**encils each **B**oy has

P_G the number of **P**encils each **G**irl has

L the cost of **L**unch for each student (in cents)

S the cost of a **S**nack for each student (in cents)

M the amount of time each student spends in **M**ath class per day (in minutes)

E the amount of time each student spends in **E**nglish class per day (in minutes)

H_M the amount of time that each student spends on **H**omework for **M**ath per day (in minutes)

H_E the amount of time that each student spends on **H**omework for **E**nglish per day (in minutes)

1. What, if anything, does each of the following algebraic expressions represent? (Use a summary phrase, if possible.)

   a. $B + G$

   b. GP_G

   c. $BM + BH_M$

   d. LS

2. Write an algebraic expression for each of the phrases below.

   a. The total number of pencils for the students in the class

   b. The cost of lunch for the whole class

   c. The total amount of time that the students in the class spend on English each day (both in class and on homework)

3. Make up some other meaningful expressions using the list of variables above.

Variables of Your Own

1. Make up a set of between five and ten variables for a situation, the way you did in *Ox Expressions.*

   You might choose something like Marching Band Expressions, Baseball Game Expressions, Dating Expressions, or Clothing Store Expressions, or you might prefer to make up a situation of your own.

   On the front of a sheet of paper, write down your variables and what they stand for.

2. Below your list of variables, write three algebraic expressions using your variables for which someone can write a summary phrase.

   On the back of the same sheet of paper, write a summary phrase for each of your algebraic expressions.

3. On the front side of the paper, write three summary phrases for which someone can write an algebraic expression using your variables.

   On the back side, write an algebraic expression for each of your summary phrases.

When you are ready, you will exchange papers with other students. Your task will then be to find summary phrases for each other's algebraic expressions and algebraic expressions for each other's summary phrases.

Integers Only

In *Homework 10: If I Could See This Thing,* you developed a formula for the number of people who would die on the trail between Fort Kearny and Fort Laramie.

You may have wondered about the fact that this formula perhaps showed 1.7 people dying, or a number like that which didn't make any sense.

Continued on next page

Interactive Mathematics Program

299

There are many problems where the function involved should only give whole number outputs or only give integer outputs. Mathematicians have invented a special function and notation for dealing with such situations.

The function is called the **greatest integer function**. If the input to this function is represented by the letter N, the output is represented by the notation $[N]$.

This function is defined by "rounding down" the input, which means choosing the integer that is as large as possible without being larger than the input. If the input is already an integer, no rounding is needed. For example:

$$[7.2] = 7$$

$$[3] = 3$$

$$[-3.3] = -4 \text{ (Remember that } -3 \text{ is bigger than } -3.3.)$$

1. Which of the statements below are true? If you think a statement is false, give a specific counterexample. If you think a statement is true, prove it as best you can.

   a. $[x + y] = [x] + [y]$

   b. $[x + 5] = [x] + 5$

   c. $[-x] = -[x]$

2. Draw the graph of the function defined by the rule $Out = [In]$.

The Overland Trail   Supplemental Problem

Movin' West

The westward movement of people across the continent began well before the Overland Trail era.

In fact, the United States population has been moving westward since the earliest years of the country.

The "population center of gravity" of the United States is the point at which the country would balance if it were looked at as a flat plate with no weight of its own and every person on it had equal weight.

In 1790, this center of gravity was near Baltimore, Maryland. In 1990, it crossed the Mississippi River to Steelville, Missouri (southwest of St. Louis).

1. From 1950 until today, the population center of gravity has moved about 50 miles west for every 10 years.

   Suppose this pattern continues for a while. Find a rule that expresses approximately how many miles west of Steelville the population center of gravity would be when it is x years after 1990.

2. Steelville is about 700 miles west of Baltimore. (It is also slightly south, but ignore that.)

   How does the rate of westward movement of the center of gravity between 1790 and 1950 compare to its rate from 1950 to 1990? Explain your answer carefully.

3. How long do you think the rule you found in Question 1 could continue to hold true? How do you think it might change?

Spilling the Beans

Three travelers met one night along the Overland Trail, and decided to have dinner together.

Sam had seven cans of beans to contribute and Kara contributed five cans of beans. Jock didn't have any beans, but the three cooked up what they had, and each ate the same amount.

After dinner, Jock offered the 84¢ in his pocket and said that the other two could divide it up in an appropriate way. They all agreed that in this way everyone would have contributed a fair share to the dinner.

Jock thought that Kara's share of the money should be 35¢, but Sam and Kara convinced him that this was wrong.

1. Explain why Jock might have thought that Kara's share was 35¢.

2. Then explain what Kara's correct share should be.

From *Mathematics: Problem Solving Through Recreational Mathematics* by Averbach and Chein. Copyright © 1980 by W.H. Freeman and Company. Adapted with permission.

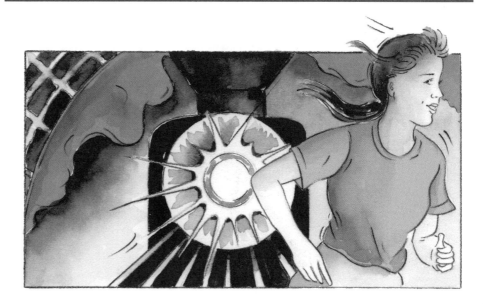

The Perils of Pauline

In 1869, the transcontinental railroad was completed. People could then travel westward by train instead of by covered wagon. But trains could also be dangerous.

One day, for example, Pauline was walking through a train tunnel on her way to town. Suddenly, she heard the whistle of a train approaching from behind her!

Pauline knew that the train always traveled at an even 60 miles per hour. She also knew that she was exactly three-eighths of the way through the tunnel, and she could tell from the train whistle how far the train was from the tunnel.

Pauline wasn't sure if she should run forward as fast as she could, or run back to the near end of the tunnel.

Well, she did some lightning-fast calculations, based on how fast she could run and the length of the tunnel. She figured out that whichever way she ran, she would just barely make it out of the tunnel before the train reached her. Whew!!!

How fast could Pauline run? (Carefully explain how you found the answer.)

High-Low Proofs

You may have come up with some interesting observations as you investigated
POW 11: High-Low Differences.

But perhaps it's still a mystery to you why high-low differences work the way they do.

In this activity, you are to *prove* as many observations about high-low differences as you
can.

Although you may want to use specific examples to illustrate your thinking, try to make
your arguments as general as possible.

Appendix B
Blackline Masters

For many of the discussions in this unit, you will find it helpful to have overhead transparencies of various diagrams. This appendix contains copies of these diagrams for your use in making such transparencies.

- Large versions of graphs from Questions 1–4 of *Wagon Train Sketches and Situations* (Day 11)

- Large versions of graphs from Questions 1–4 of *Homework 11: Graph Sketches*

- Large versions of graphs form Questions 1–3 of *Out Numbered* (Day 13)

- Large versions of maps from *Homework 15: Broken Promises* (5 maps altogether)

This appendix also contains copies of the in-class and take-home assessments for the unit and a first semester final assessment (four pages) suggested for schools using a traditional semester schedule. The semester assessment is designed on the assumption that your class will have studied the first two units, *Patterns* and *The Game of Pig*, and the beginning of the third unit, *The Overland Trail*. This semester assessment is not intended to be a comprehensive test of the material in these units, but focuses instead on some essential ideas.

We recommend that you give students two hours for this semester assessment so they can complete it without time pressure, and that you allow them to use graphing calculators and to have access to their textbooks and notes (including portfolios).

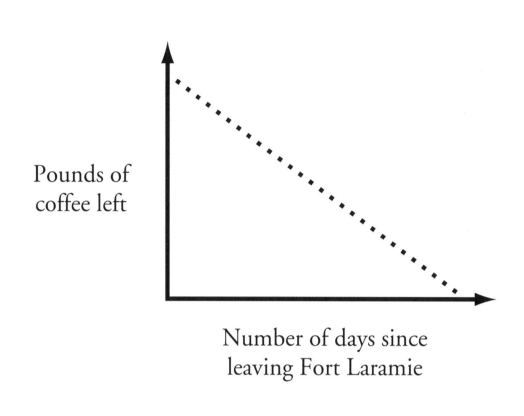

Pounds of coffee left

Number of days since leaving Fort Laramie

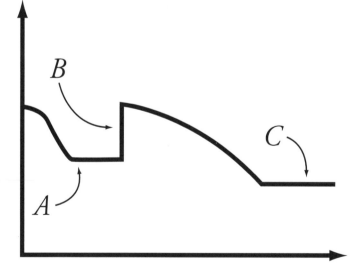

Amount of water in storage on the wagon

Distance from Fort Laramie

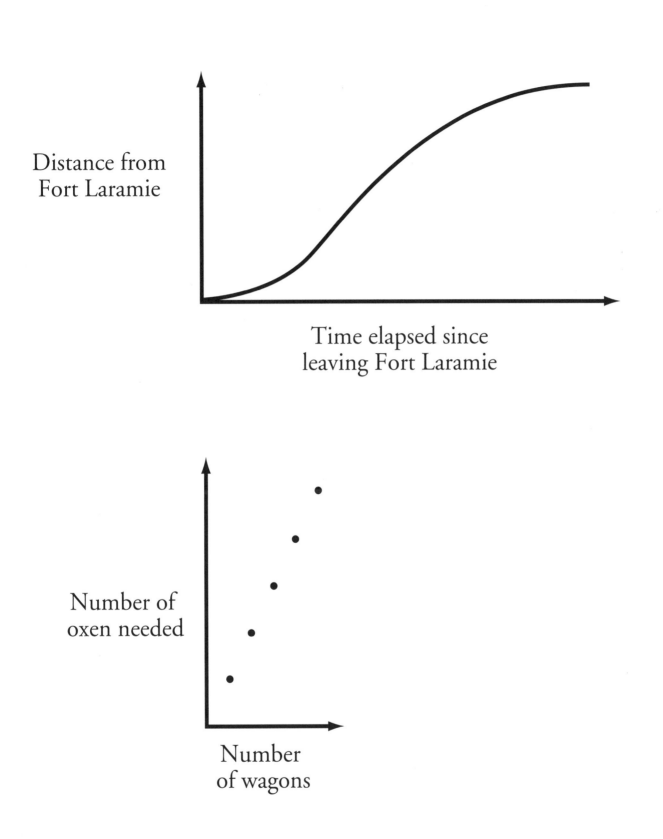

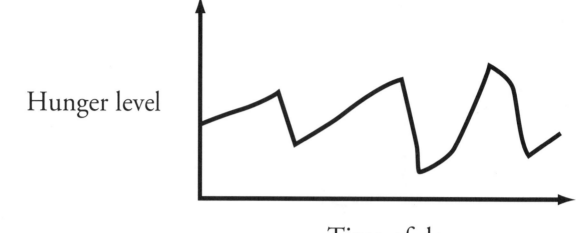

Hunger level

Time of day

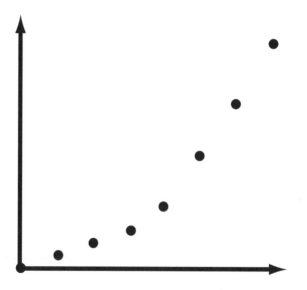

Percent of POW completed by the end of the day

Number of days since POW was assigned

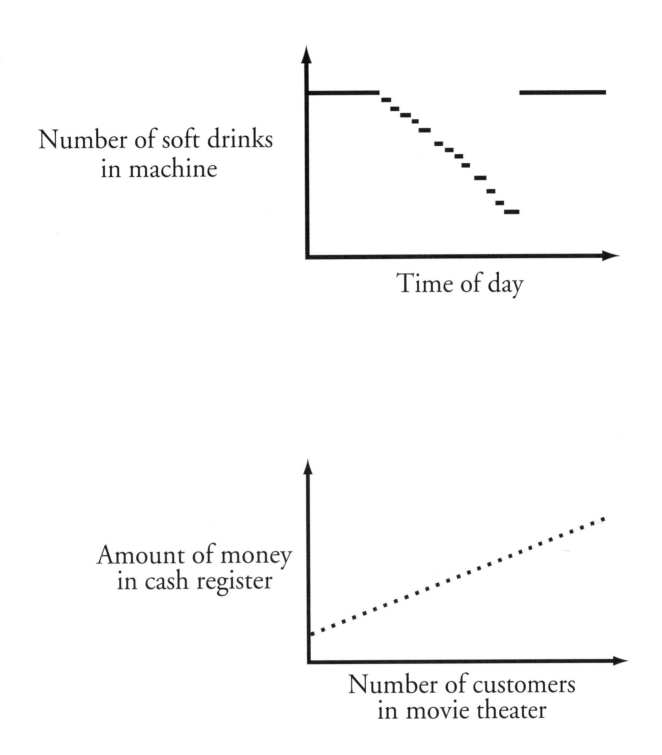

Number of soft drinks
in machine

Time of day

Amount of money
in cash register

Number of customers
in movie theater

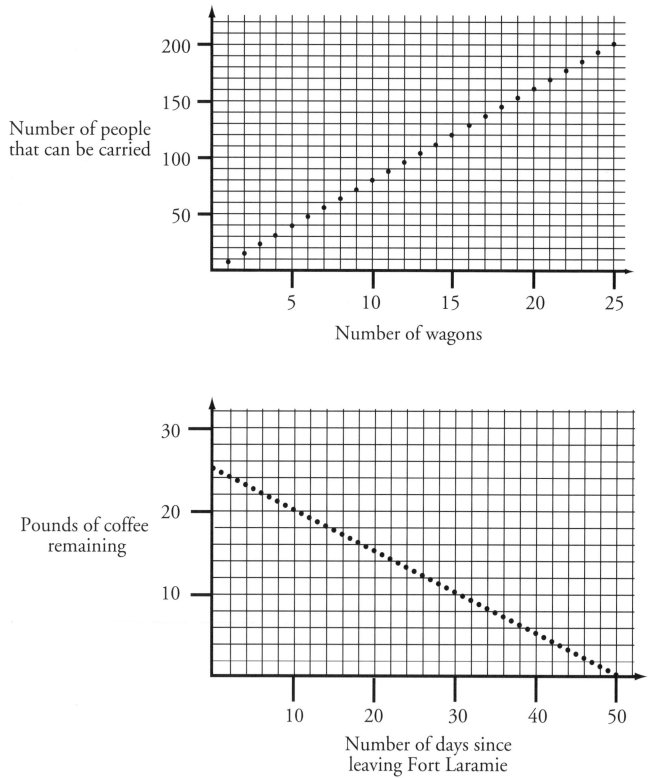

Number of people that can be carried

Number of wagons

Pounds of coffee remaining

Number of days since leaving Fort Laramie

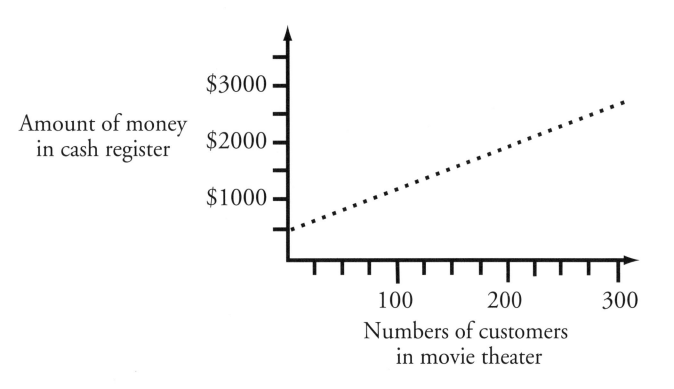

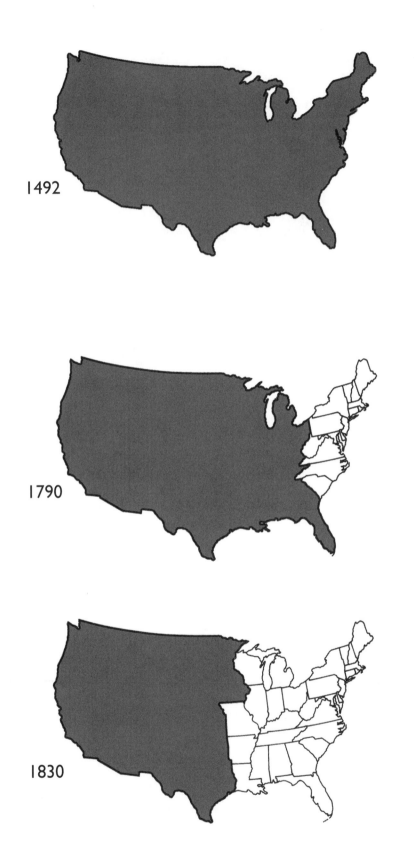

1492

1790

1830

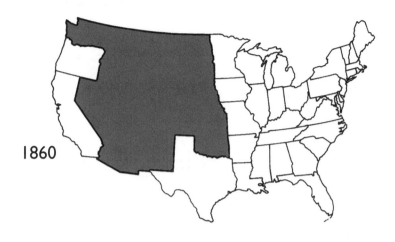

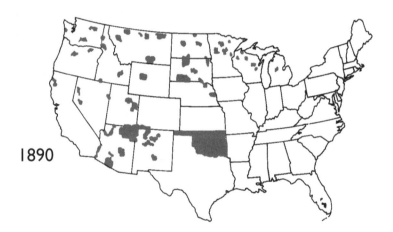

In-Class Assessment for "The Overland Trail"

The questions in this assessment are about a modern-day move from Kansas City, Missouri, to San Francisco, California.

Unlike the settlers of 1850, your family will travel on superhighways with a large rental truck and a van. The distance between the two cities is 1500 miles.

In answering the questions, be sure to show your reasoning, not just give an answer. Assume that your average speed is 50 miles per hour.

1. Suppose you estimate that you can drive for an average of six hours on a typical day of the trip. How many days will the trip last at this rate?

2. Construct an In-Out table in which the *In* column contains the number of hours of driving per day and the *Out* column shows how many days the trip will last.

3. Plot the points from your table in Question 2, to show the number of days in the trip as a function of how many hours you are willing to drive per day.

4. Create an algebraic expression that shows how to compute the number of days required for a trip like this (not necessarily 1500 miles—you should represent the distance by a variable). This expression should not contain any numbers and you should clearly define the symbols in it.

Take-Home Assessment for
The Overland Trail

As in the *In-Class Assessment for "The Overland Trail,"* the questions below have to do with a modern-day move.

Your family is traveling on superhighways with a large rental truck and a van.

1. *Fuel Economies*

Each time one of the vehicles stops for gas, you make a note of how much gas the vehicle has used and how many miles it has traveled.

    a. Using the data in the tables below, draw two graphs *on the same set of axes*, comparing total miles traveled to total gallons of gas used for each vehicle:

<table>
<thead>
<tr><th colspan="2">Van</th><th colspan="2">Truck</th></tr>
<tr>
<th>Total amount amount of gas used so far</th>
<th>Total number of miles traveled so far</th>
<th>Total amount amount of gas used so far</th>
<th>Total number of miles traveled so far</th>
</tr>
</thead>
<tbody>
<tr><td>18</td><td>400</td><td>36</td><td>300</td></tr>
<tr><td>28</td><td>700</td><td>65</td><td>600</td></tr>
<tr><td>42</td><td>990</td><td>100</td><td>850</td></tr>
<tr><td>52</td><td>1250</td><td>138</td><td>1100</td></tr>
</tbody>
</table>

    b. Reading from the graph, estimate how many gallons of gas the truck had guzzled by the time you traveled 800 miles. And how about the van?

    c. Estimate how many miles each vehicle can travel on a gallon of gas.

2. Van Repairs

One morning, as you attempt to get started, you find that the van won't start. The garage mechanic says that the fuel pump needs replacement and that the work can be done fairly quickly, in about two hours.

The family decides that Mom and you should head out in the truck towards that night's stop, 400 miles down the highway. Dad and the rest of the family will remain behind and either catch up with you during the day or meet you tonight at the motel where you have reservations.

a. Suppose that the truck travels at 45 miles per hour, that the van goes at 55 miles per hour (once it is fixed), and that the repair actually takes two hours. For the sake of simplicity, assume that neither vehicle makes any stops along the way.

   i. Which vehicle will get to the motel first?

   ii. How far from the motel will the other vehicle be when the first vehicle reaches the motel?

b. Of course, the repair might not take the full two hours, or it might take longer. So now consider the case where the repair actually takes four hours. (In this case, the truck definitely arrives first.)

   How far from the motel will the van be when the truck reaches the motel?

c. Now generalize from parts a and b. Suppose that h represents the number of hours of delay for the van. (Assume that h is a number large enough to allow the truck to arrive first.)

   Develop a formula or equation in terms of h that says how far the van will be from the motel when the truck arrives at the motel.

I. The Antique Probability Cubes

Sally and Alejandro are studying probability in school. One of their teachers has brought in a collection of old dice that includes two rather peculiar dice.

One of these dice has a 0 where the 4 usually is, so that its faces are 1, 2, 3, 0, 5, and 6. The other has a 0 where the 1 usually is, so its faces are 0, 2, 3, 4, 5, and 6. Like normal dice, each face has an equal chance of coming up.

The teacher has challenged Sally and Alejandro to investigate the probability of rolling various sums with these two dice.

Imagine that you are Sally or Alejandro and you have accepted this challenge.

1. Find the probability of rolling a sum of 7 with these dice. Show all work.

2. What sum would be the most likely with this pair of dice? Explain why.

II. Another Coin Game

Consider this coin game:

> You flip a coin. If the coin comes up heads, you lose, and your game is over.
>
> If the coin comes up tails, you then roll a regular die. Whatever number comes up on the die is the number of dollars you win.

1. Make an area diagram to illustrate the possible outcomes of this game and their probabilities.

2. Compute the expected value for this game, explaining your work.

3. Suppose a county fair charges you $2 each time you play the game.

   In the long run, who will come out ahead—you or the county fair? By how much per game? Explain your answer.

4. Suppose a law is passed that says that the county fair's profit cannot average more than 20¢ per game. Give a specific way to change the game so that the fair could still make a profit charging $2 per game.

III. Field Trip Expressions

The following variables represent the amounts of different things related to a class field trip to a museum. Examine this list of variable names.

V	the number of buses the school district has
F	the number of buses used for the field trip
B	the number of boys on each bus
G	the number of girls on each bus
M	the number of miles to the museum
P	the number miles per gallon each bus gets
C	the cost of a gallon of gas
T	the number of teachers on each bus
S	the number of gallons of gas that the gas tank for a bus will hold
D	the cost per person of admission to the museum

1. What, if anything, do the following expressions represent? (Use a summary phrase, if possible.)

   a. $B + G$

   b. TV

   c. CSV

2. Write an expression for each of these summary phrases.

   a. The amount of money the museum will collect from the field trip

   b. The number of buses that did not go on the field trip

   c. The cost of gas for the field trip

3. Make up a "field trip expression" of your own using the list of variables above, and explain what it means.

IV. Mini-POW

Solve this problem. Then write up your results, describing your process and solution as you would for a Problem of the Week.

Consider this sequence of diagrams.

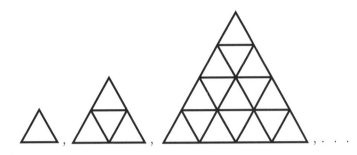

The first diagram is made up of three line segments of equal length. You can think of the second diagram as made up of nine segments of that same length, and so on.

1. Find the number of segments of the given length that would be needed for the 10th diagram in this sequence.

2. Explain how you would find the number of segments of the given length that would be needed for the 100th diagram in this sequence.

Glossary

This is the glossary for all five units of IMP Year 1.

Absolute value   The distance a number is from 0 on the number line. The symbol | | stands for absolute value.

Examples: $|-2| = 2$; $|7| = 7$; $|0| = 0$

Acute angle   An angle that measures more than 0° and less than 90°.

Acute triangle   A triangle whose angles are all acute.

Adjacent angles   Two angles with the same vertex and formed using a shared ray.

Example: Angles *A* and *B* are adjacent angles.

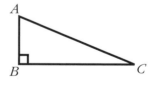

Adjacent side   (for an acute angle of a right triangle) The side of the right triangle which, together with the hypotenuse, forms the given angle.

Example: In the right triangle *ABC,* side $\overline{BC}$ is adjacent to $\angle C$, and side $\overline{AB}$ is adjacent to $\angle A$.

Alternate interior angles   If two lines are intersected by a transversal, then the inside angles that are on opposite sides of the transversal are alternate interior angles.

Example: Angles K and L are one pair of alternate interior angles, and angles M and N are another pair.

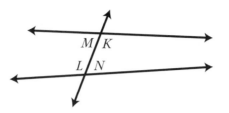

Amplitude

(for a pendulum) The angle of a pendulum's swing, measured from the vertical to the most outward position of the pendulum during its swing.

Example: The pendulum in the diagram has an amplitude of 20°.

Angle

Informally, an amount of turn, usually measured in **degrees.** Formally, the geometric figure formed by two **rays** with a common initial point, called the **vertex** of the angle.

Angle of elevation

The angle at which an object appears above the horizontal, as measured from a chosen point.

Example: The diagram shows the angle of elevation to the top of the tree from point A.

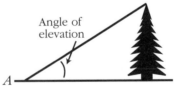

Area

Informally, the amount of space inside a two-dimensional figure, usually measured in square units.

Area model

For probability, a diagram showing the possible outcomes of a particular event. Each portion of the model represents an outcome, and the ratio of the area of that portion to the area of the whole model is the probability of that outcome.

Axis	(plural: **axes**) See **Coordinate system.**
Coefficient	Usually, a number being used to multiply a variable or power of a variable in an algebraic expression.
	Example: In the expression $3x + 4x^2$, 3 and 4 are coefficients.
Complementary angles	A pair of angles whose measures add to 90°. If two complementary angles are adjacent, together they form a right angle.
Composite number	A counting number having more than two whole-number divisors.
	Example: 12 is a composite number because it has the divisors 1, 2, 3, 4, 6, and 12.
Conclusion	Informally, any statement arrived at by reasoning or through examples.
	See also **"If . . . , then . . ." statement.**
Conditional probability	The probability that an event will occur based on the assumption that some other event has already occurred.
Congruent	Informally, having the same shape and size. Formally, two polygons are congruent if their corresponding angles have equal measure and their corresponding sides are equal in length. The symbol ≅ means "is congruent to."
Conjecture	A theory or an idea about how something works, usually based on examples.
Constraint	Informally, a limitation or restriction.
Continuous graph	Informally, a graph that can be drawn without lifting the pencil, in contrast to a **discrete graph.**
Coordinate system	A way to represent points in the plane with pairs of numbers called **coordinates.** The system is based on

two perpendicular lines, one horizontal and one vertical, called **coordinate axes.** The point where the lines meet is called the **origin.** Traditionally, the axes are labeled with the variables x and y as shown below. The horizontal axis is often called the **x-axis** and the vertical axis is often called the **y-axis.**

Example: Point A has coordinates $(3, -2)$.

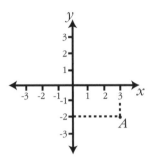

Corresponding angles

(for a transversal) If two lines are intersected by a transversal, then two angles are corresponding angles if they occupy the same position relative to the transversal and the other lines that form them.

Example: Angles A and D are a pair of corresponding angles, and angles B and E are another pair of corresponding angles.

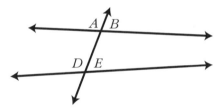

Corresponding parts

For a pair of similar or congruent polygons, sides or angles of the two polygons that have the same relative position.

Example: Side a in the small triangle and side b in the large triangle are corresponding parts.

Counterexample   An example which demonstrates that a conjecture is not true.

Degree   The measurement unit for an angle defined by having a complete turn equal to 360 degrees. The symbol ° represents degrees.

Diagonal   In a polygon, a line segment that connects two vertices and that is not a side of the polygon.

Discrete graph   A graph consisting of isolated or unconnected points, in contrast to a **continuous graph.**

Divisor   A factor of an integer.

Example: 1, 2, 3, 4, 6, and 12 are the positive divisors of 12.

Domain   The set of values that can be used as inputs for a given function.

Equilateral triangle   A triangle with all sides the same length.

Expected value   In a game or other probability situation, the average amount gained or lost per turn in the long run.

Exterior angle   An angle formed outside a polygon by extending one of its sides.

Example: The diagram shows an exterior angle for polygon *ABCDE.*

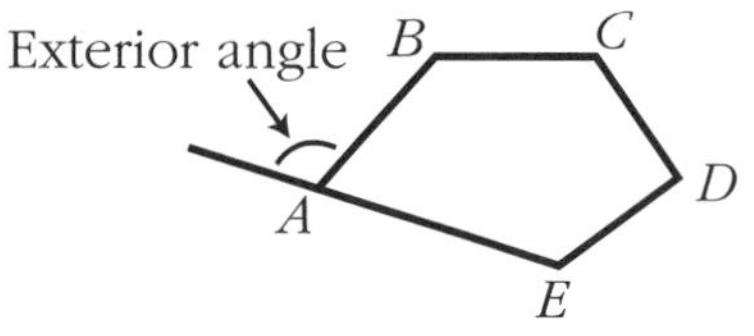

Exterior angle

Factor   The same as **divisor.**

Factorial   The product of all the whole numbers from a particular number down to 1. The symbol ! stands for factorial.

Example: 5! (read "five factorial") means $5 \cdot 4 \cdot 3 \cdot 2 \cdot 1$.

Fair game   A game in which both players are expected to come out equally well in the long run.

Frequency bar graph

A bar graph showing how often each result occurs.

Example: This frequency bar graph shows, for instance, that 11 times in 80 rolls, the sum of two dice was 6.

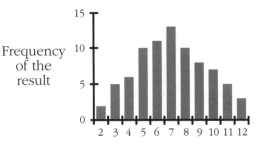

Function

Informally, a process or rule for determining the numerical value of one variable in terms of another. A function is often represented as a set of number pairs in which the second number is determined by the first, according to the function rule.

Graph

A mathematical diagram for displaying information.

Hexagon

A polygon with six sides.

Hypotenuse

The longest side in a right triangle, or the length of this side. The hypotenuse is located opposite the right angle.

Example: In right triangle *ABC,* the hypotenuse is $\overline{AC}$.

Hypothesis

Informally, a theory about a situation or about how a certain set of data is behaving. Also, a set of assumptions being used to analyze or understand a situation.

See also **"If . . . , then . . ." statement.**

"If . . . , then . . ." statement

A specific form of mathematical statement, saying that if one condition is true, then another condition must also be true.

Example: Here is a true "If . . . , then . . ." statement.

If two angles of a triangle have equal measure, then the sides opposite these angles have equal length.

The condition "two angles of a triangle have equal measure" is the **hypothesis.** The condition "the sides opposite these angles have equal length" is the **conclusion.**

Independent events

Two (or more) events are independent if the outcome of one does not influence the outcome of the other.

Integer

Any number that is either a counting number, zero, or the opposite of a counting number. The integers can be represented using set notation as

$$\{\,\ldots -3, -2, -1, 0, 1, 2, 3, \ldots \}$$

Examples: $-4, 0$, and 10 are integers.

Interior angle

An angle inside a figure, especially within a polygon.

Example: Angle *BAE* is an interior angle of the polygon *ABCDE*.

Interior angle

Isosceles triangle

A triangle with two sides of equal length.

Leg

Either of the two shorter sides in a right triangle. The two legs of a right triangle form the right angle of the triangle. The longest side of a right triangle (the hypotenuse) is not considered a leg.

Line of best fit

Informally, the line that comes closest to fitting a given set of points on a discrete graph.

Line segment

The portion of a straight line between two given points.

Mathematical model

A mathematical description or structure used to represent how a real-life situation works.

Mean

The numerical average of a data set, found by adding the data items and dividing by the number of items in the set.

Example: For the data set 8, 12, 12, 13, and 17, the sum of the data items is 62 and there are 5 items in the data set, so the mean is 62 ÷ 5, or 12.4.

Measurement variation

The situation of taking several measurements of the same thing and getting different results.

Median

(of a set of data) The "middle number" in a set of data that has been arranged from smallest to largest.

Example: For the data set 4, 17, 22, 56, and 100, the median is 22, because it is the number in the middle of the list.

Mode

(of a set of data) The number that occurs most often in a set of data. Many sets of data do not have a single mode.

Example: For the data set 3, 4, 7, 16, 18, 18, and 23, the mode is 18.

Natural number   Any of the counting numbers 1, 2, 3, 4, and so on.

Normal distribution

A certain precisely defined set of probabilities, which can often be used to approximate real-life events. Sometimes used to refer to any data set whose frequency bar graph is approximately "bell-shaped."

Observed probability

The likelihood of a certain event happening based on observed results, as distinct from **theoretical probability.**

Obtuse angle

An angle that measures more than 90° and less than 180°.

Obtuse triangle   A triangle with an obtuse angle.

Octagon   An eight-sided polygon.

Opposite side   The side of a triangle across from a given angle.

Order of operations

A set of conventions that mathematicians have agreed to use whenever a calculation involves more than one operation.

Example: 2 + 3 · 4 is 14, not 20, because the conventions for order of operations tell us to multiply before we add.

Ordered pair   Two numbers paired together using the format *(x, y)*, often used to locate a point in the coordinate system.

Origin   See **Coordinate system.**

Parallel lines   Two lines in a plane that do not intersect.

Pentagon   A five-sided polygon.

Perimeter   The boundary of a polygon, or the total length of this boundary.

Period   The length of time for a cyclical event to complete one full cycle.

Perpendicular lines   A pair of lines that form a right angle.

Polygon   A closed two-dimensional shape formed by three or more line segments. The line segments that form a polygon are called its sides. The endpoints of these segments are called **vertices** (singular: **vertex**).

Examples: All the figures below are polygons.

Prime number   A whole number greater than 1 that has only two whole number divisors, 1 and itself.

Example: 7 is a prime number, because its only whole number divisors are 1 and 7.

Probability   The likelihood of a certain event happening. For a situation involving equally likely outcomes, the probability that the outcome of an event will be an outcome within a given set is defined by a ratio:

$$\text{Probability} = \frac{\text{number of outcomes in the set}}{\text{total number of possible outcomes}}$$

Example: If a die has 2 red faces and 4 green faces, the probability of getting a green face is

$$\frac{\text{number of green faces}}{\text{total number of faces}} = \frac{4}{6}$$

Proof   An absolutely convincing argument.

Proportion   A statement that two ratios are equal.

Proportional   Having the same ratio.

Example: Corresponding sides of triangles *ABC* and *DEF* are proportional, because the ratios $\frac{4}{6}$, $\frac{8}{12}$, and $\frac{10}{15}$ are equal.

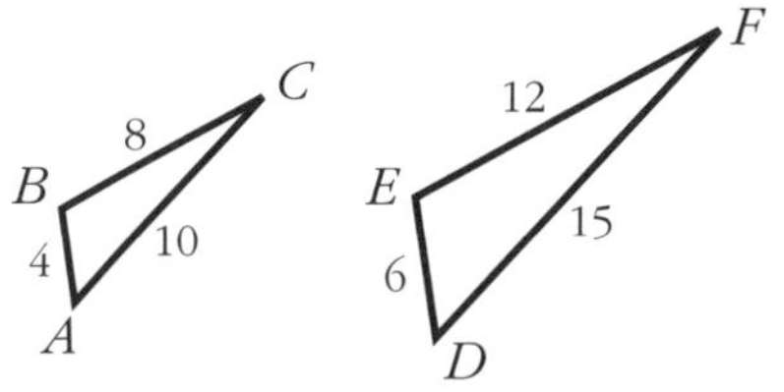

Quadrant   One of the four areas created in a coordinate system by using the *x*-axis and the *y*-axis as boundaries. The quadrants have standard numbering as shown below.

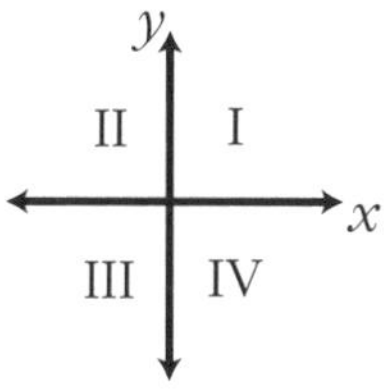

Quadrilateral   A four-sided polygon.

Random   Used in probability to indicate that any of several events is equally likely or that an event is selected from a set of events according to a precisely described distribution.

Range   (of a set of data) The difference between the largest and smallest numbers in the set.

Example: For the data set 7, 12, 18, 18, and 29, the range is 29 – 7, or 22.

Ray   The part of a line from a single point, called the **vertex,** through another point on the line and continuing infinitely in that direction.

Rectangle	A four-sided polygon whose angles are all right angles.
Regular polygon	A polygon whose sides all have equal length and whose angles all have equal measure.
Rhombus	A four-sided polygon whose sides all have the same length.
Right angle	An angle that measures 90°.
Right triangle	A triangle with a right angle.
Sample standard deviation	The calculation on a set of data taken from a larger population of data, used to estimate the standard deviation of the larger population.
Sequence	A list of numbers or expressions, usually following a pattern or rule. Example: 1, 3, 5, 7, 9, . . . is the sequence of positive odd numbers.
Similar	Informally, having the same shape. Formally, two polygons are similar if their corresponding angles have equal measure and their corresponding sides are proportional in length. The symbol ~ means "is similar to."
Simulation	An experiment or set of experiments using a model of a certain event that is based on the same probabilities as the real event. Simulations allow people to estimate the likelihood of an event when it is impractical to experiment with the real event.
Slope	Informally, the steepness of a line.
Solution	A number that, when substituted for a variable in an equation, makes the equation a true statement. Example: The value $x = 3$ is a solution to the equation $2x = 6$ because $2 \cdot 3 = 6$.
Square	A four-sided polygon with all sides of equal length and with four right angles.

Square root   A number whose square is a given number. The symbol $\sqrt{\ }$ is used to denote the nonnegative square root of a number.

Example: Both 6 and –6 are square roots of 36, because $6^2 = 36$ and $(-6)^2 = 36$; $\sqrt{36} = 6$.

Standard deviation   A specific measurement of how spread out a set of data is, usually represented by the lowercase Greek letter sigma (σ).

Straight angle   An angle that measures 180°. The rays forming a straight angle together make up a straight line.

Strategy   A complete plan about how to proceed in a game or problem situation. A strategy for a game should tell a person exactly what to do under any situation that can arise in the game.

Supplementary angles   A pair of angles whose measures add to 180°. If two supplementary angles are adjacent, together they form a straight angle.

Term   (of an algebraic expression) A part of an algebraic expression, combined with other terms using addition or subtraction.

Example: The expression $2x^2 + 3x - 12$ has three terms: $2x^2$, $3x$, and 12.

Term   (of a sequence) One of the items listed in a sequence.

Example: In the sequence 3, 5, 7, . . . , the number 3 is the first term, 5 is the second term, and so on.

Theoretical probability   The likelihood of an event occurring, as explained by a theory or model, as distinct from **observed probability.**

Transversal   A line that intersects two or more other lines.

Example: The line *l* is a transversal that intersects the lines *m* and *n*.

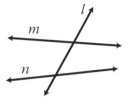

Trapezoid	A four-sided polygon with exactly one pair of parallel sides.

Example: Quadrilateral *PQRS* is a trapezoid, because $\overline{QR}$ and $\overline{PS}$ are parallel and $\overline{PQ}$ and $\overline{SR}$ are not parallel.

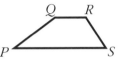

Triangle	A polygon with three sides.
Triangle inequality principle	The principle that the lengths of any two sides of a triangle must add up to more than the length of the third side.
Trigonometric function	Any of six functions defined for acute angles in terms of ratios of sides of a right triangle.
Vertex	(plural: **vertices**) See **Angle, Polygon,** and **Ray.**
Vertical angles	A pair of "opposite" angles formed by a pair of intersecting lines.

Example: Angles *F* and *G* are vertical angles.

Whole number	A number that is either zero or a counting number.
x-intercept	A place on a graph where a line or curve crosses the *x*-axis.
y-intercept	A place on a graph where a line or curve crosses the *y*-axis.

Photographic Credits

Teacher Book Classroom Photography

8 Thurgood Marshall Academic High School, Lynne Alper; **12** Thurgood Marshall Academic High School, Lynne Alper; **27** Encinal High School, Lynne Alper; **44** Capuchino High School, Lynne Alper; **129** Capuchino High School, Lynne Alper.

Student Book Classroom Photography

3 Lincoln High School, Lori Green; **14** Lincoln High School, Lori Green; **27** Lincoln High School, Lori Green; **36** Lincoln High School, Lori Green; **42** San Lorenzo Valley High School, Kim Gough; **55** Lincoln High School, Lori Green; **95** Foothill High School, Sheryl Dozier; **104** Foothill High School, Sheryl Dozier; **114** Mendocino Community High School, Lynne Alper; **127** Mendocino High School, Lynne Alper; **150** Lake View High School, Carol Caref; **157** West High School, Janice Bussey; **189** Whitney Young High School, Carol Berland; **210** Pleasant Valley High School, Michael Christensen; **222** Lynne Alper; **238** East Bakersfield High School, Susan Lloyd; **252** Lincoln High School, Lynne Alper; **274** Colton High School, Sharon Taylor; **281** Foothill High School, Sheryl Dozier; **307** Santa Cruz High School, Lynne Alper; **324** Foothill High School, Cheryl Dozier; **352** Santa Maria High School, Mike Bryant; **366** Santa Cruz High School, Lynne Alper; **373** Shasta High School, Dave Robathan; **397** Santa Cruz High School, Lynne Alper; **414** Santa Maria High School, Mike Bryant; **424** Bartram Communications Academy, Robert Powlen; **446** Santa Maria High School, Mike Bryant; **460** Ranum High School, Rita Quintana

Front Cover Students

Tamalpais High School, Katrina Van Loan, Jenee Desmond, David Trammell, Gina Uriarte, Thea Singleton, Itan Novis, Sarah N. Weintraub photographed by Hilary Turner